C000257643

CIDER-
THE FORGOTTEN MIRACLE

The Great Cyder Press. See Treatise on Cyder making

CIDER-
THE FORGOTTEN MIRACLE

James Crowden

CYDER PRESS 2

This book is dedicated to my father who has always been a great support in all my ventures and is pretty handy when it comes to a bit of research, which can often involve sitting out in the garden, testing a drop of good farmhouse cider...

First published in October 1999 by Cyder Press 2

The Old Parsonage, Somerton, Somerset TA11 7PF

Text and poems © James Crowden 1999
Cover illutration © Brian Hanscomb 1979
Photograph © George Wright 1996

ISBN   0 9537103 0 0

A CIP copy of this book is available
from the British Library

Printed by Bigwood & Staple, Bridgwater

This book was written, designed, printed
and published in Somerset

Contents

Acknowledgments

First of all I should acknowledge the help of those who have in some way contributed to getting the book off the ground. It has long been in my mind to do such a book. Such is the way with books until they gain their own inner momentum. My main thanks must go to Sue Clifford and Angela King of Common Ground who have over the last year employed me on a retainer as their *'Apple Day'* Poet and have in fact given me the very obvious deadline of Apple Day 1999 to aim for. To Jane Kendall and Dan Keech also of Common Ground for reams of information about apples all over the country, which has certainly focused my mind on orchards and cider wonderfully.

I am very grateful to Julian Temperley for the loan of his copy of John Worlidge's *VINETUM BRITTANICUM or a TREATISE ON CIDER* 1678 edition and for employing me over the last dozen years on a casual basis during the autumn in the Burrow Hill Cider House, which you could call a *'pressing engagement'*. To Nick Sloan for the loan of his copy of *'THE CYDER POEM'* by John Phillips, 1727 edition, and for his advice on typography, illustration and layout. To David Walker of Somerset Rural Life Museum, Glastonbury for access to the cider records and other information collected by Philippa Legg and Hilary Binding deposited there during research for their excellent book *'Somerset Cider – The Complete Story'* published by Somerset Books, which was a great help and inspiration. To Peter Irvine of Dorset Record Office for some choice bits of information about *'scrumping'* in the Sturminster Newton area circa 1846, as well as for pointing me in the right direction for the *Poor Law Reports* and the conditions of Women and Children in Agriculture. To John Cluett for his recollections of cider and the 'Apple Trains'. To Richard Budd of Hinton St George for his priceless 'nuggets of

history' dug up by the Dinnington Docks Historical Society... To Pedair MacNeice of Armagh for information about the 'Irish' bog apple. To David Prysor-Jones for research and loan of cider books. To Jonathan and Sara Hudston for editorial advice and much needed rigorous proof reading.

Grateful acknowledgement is given to all those who have given permission in one way for various extracts to be used within the book. To RKP for permission to use the extracts from *'The Prose of John Clare'* edited by JW & Anne Tibble. To John Fowles for permission to use the extract from *'The Tree'* first published by the Aurum Press, To Common Ground, not only for the extract from their essay *'The Apple, the Orchard, the Cultural Landscape'*, but for small items of apple information from their two books, *'The Apple Source Book'* and *'Apple Games and Customs'*. To Robert Hale for the extract from *'The History and Virtues of Cyder'* by RK French. To Orion and David & Charles in attempts to find out the copyright for the extract from AK Hamilton Jenkin's *'Cornwall & the Cornish'*, first published by JM Dent. To Farrar Strauss & Giroux for permission to use Frank Browning's quote from his book *'Apples'* published New York 1998. Also to Harper Collins for trying to trace the copyright on WG Hoskins and Pollard and Beech. Other shorter extracts and quotes have come from *'The Book of Apples'* by Joan Morgan & Alison Richards, The Hakluyt Society for extracts from *'Newfoundland Discovered : Richard Whitbourne's Discourse'* by Gillian T Cell. *'Cider and Folklore'* by Walter Minchinton. *'The Golden Bough'* by Sir James Frazer MacMillan Press 1922. Extracts about *Champagne* have come from Tom Stevenson's book of the same name published by Absolute Press and Christies. Extracts for *'Sir Kenelm Digby's Closet Opened'* have come from a recent reprint published by Prospect Books and edited with an excellent foreword by Jane Stevenson and Peter Davidson. One or two nuggets of Somerset history have come from

Robin Bush's 'Somerset-The Complete Guide' published by The Dovecote Press. With one or two other quotes, I have tried very hard to find the owners of the copyright, but without success. In these days of ultimate computerisation, anything that is not on disk does not 'exist'... If any are found to be wanting, the error is mine and I would be grateful if they could get in touch if that were necessary.

My thanks must also go to Chris Staple and his staff for their patience and skill in the Design & Printing departments of *Bigwood & Staple* based in Bridgwater and particularly to Steve Browning who has had to make do with countless last minute alterations. By coincidence he worked for over 20 years with Taunton Cider and has himself put up many cheeses, so he knows what five hundred tons of cider apples looks like. To Richard Watkins for producing an old but very interesting illustration of a Cyder Press, as well as a great wodge of Cider Acts... To Brian Hanscomb R.E. for permission to use his engraving *'Adam and Eve in Somerset'* on the front cover and lastly and most importantly to Sue Bell for her endless support, patience and obvious good nature in letting a writer use her attic...

James Crowden
Autumn Equinox 1999

Yet is there not any drink known to us generally palatable as cider: for you may make it sute almost with any humorous drinker : it may be made luscious by an addition of a quantity of sweet apples in the first operation, pleasant being made with *Pippins* or *Gennet-Moyles* only: racy, poignant, oyly, spicy with the *Redstreaks* and other sorts of fruits, even as the Operator pleases. And it satisfies thirst, if not too stale, more than any other usual drink whatsoever.

John Worlidge   *Treatise on Cider* 1678

xi

Yet this Wine, i.e. Cyder, being that which incites some to speak too much, will I hope beg my excuse and speak for itself. It being one of the best and most advantageous pieces of improvement of our Country farms yet known...

John Worlidge   1678

Their Orchards might well be styled their Temples, and Apple Trees their Idols of Worship...

William Marshall 1796

Unlike beer, cider has a neglected history...

Walter Minchinton   1975

Introduction

Somerset Cider - The Overview

Somerset Cider is without doubt some of the finest in the world. Here on the small farms that surround the Somerset Levels and Moors, the art of cider making has the status of an ancient religion, where superstition and belief are inextricably entwined with the landscape of myth and legend, as if the fermentation was regarded with veneration, like some kind of miracle, which in a sense it is. As if in the dark of the cider house itself, they were in touch with invisible forces, only half tamed, another world dimly perceived, as if there were some kind of process at work beneath the skin, not just of the farmer, but of the apple itself.

It is a land of migrations, of summer settlers. The *Sumorsetae*, who came down from the low hills and ridges, grazed the rich green pastures with their cattle and sheep, and when the winter's flood waters came, retreated once more with their animals to the higher ground. It was here that they built the villages we see today and planted the orchards, that became the nerve centre of the community.

Good cider farms are worshipped for many miles and in the autumn the faithful congregation home in on the barn as if it were a wayside chapel or a place of pilgrimage. They inspect the sacrificial altar carefully and watch every move, just to get a bit of the action.

"As the press pushes home the life blood of the heathen apple
flows ever more freely the stout cheese dripping
ruddy brown and golden like honey
a river in flood a hive of fruit
whole orchards pulped and crushed."

Oak barrels are admired and touched just to make sure that they are not a mirage, some figment of their imagination, or worse still plastic. The names of certain apples and orchards are revered, and repeated like a mantra, the cider tested, held up to the light, sipped, run round the mouth, the palate tickled, downed, admired. Glasses and gossip are topped up, barrels tapped, and the order made. Communion with the Apple God.

For centuries apples have formed the backbone of the rural economy and the maintenance of good orchards was foremost in the farmer's mind, for without good cider, he could not attract a steady workforce. The ration for a strong man was four to six pints a day and at least half as much again at harvest. The replenishment required to keep a gang scything a field of hay or corn, was legendary. In the 1840's the ration for women was three pints and for boys aged nine, one pint a day. Your position in the pecking order was determined exactly by your ration, and you were well supervised. A better system in some ways than today, I suspect, when teenagers lace anything they can find with vodka, and even the lemonade isn't what it seems.

Overtime and rent were often paid in cider, it was a currency in times of hardship, it enabled the working man to alleviate some of the suffering of his bad wages, repetitive jobs and poor working conditions, and in time of cholera, typhus or flood, safety itself. At least you knew the water had passed through a tree trunk and was well fermented, and you only had to go to the barn to get it.

Large quantities of cider were also drunk in the cities as a cheap alternative to beer, and this provided a good outlet for much of the cider. Even in the 1970's Bristol still had at least half a dozen good cider pubs with names such as *Cotham Porter's Stores* and *The Coronation Tap*, *The White Horse* in the docks, *The Myrtle Tree* in Hotwells and *The Railway* in St Werburgh's. Unfortunately big breweries tend to dislike cider because until recently it was half or two thirds the price per pint and nearly twice as strong, arithmetic that even the most sozzled of cider drinkers can work out in a twinkling.

Beer incidentally requires not only large amounts of good water, but also fuel to boil the mash and malt the grain, as well as good barley and hops. Barley which might otherwise feed cattle or labourers in time of need. Making cider is in fact far more ecologically sound. Apples only need to be gathered and pressed, nature does the rest. And when the juice has been extracted, the pomace can be fed to hungry animals, pigs, sheep, chickens and cattle, just at the time of year when grass begins to be in short supply. Horses love apples. Cider is a simple but remarkable drink with a long pedigree, and at the end of the day, when the trees keel over in a winter storm, you have good firewood, as well as the annual pruning for kindling. Apple wood, like all fruit wood is wonderful when turned, and makes a good wood for dressers and kitchen furniture. It was also used in the early apple engines for crushing the apples, and formed the cogs between which the apples were passed, self lubricating, so to speak. Iron taints the cider and today only stainless steel should be used. Other engines used granite or gritstone rollers, in a circular trough. Perhaps these days we lose sight of our natural woods and products at our peril.

But the apple also has many other connotations within our language and has crept into many phrases. How many West Country farmers have I suspect used the expression, *"The Apple of my Eye"* when referring to their young and beautiful daughters, who no doubt, like their cider, are full of body, subtle and yet frisky. Lively is a word which springs to mind. It certainly wasn't a *Granny Smith* out the cold store that Eve had in her hand when she offered it to Adam. One in the hand is worth two in the bush orchard. Even the Serpent knew that. No. The Garden of Eden must surely have been here in the heart of Somerset. Why else would Joseph of Arimathea have come to Glastonbury, bearing especially prickly thorns to improve hedges, to keep cattle and young villains out, intent on scrumping? And don't forget William Tell. The Cross Bow versus the Long Bow or should it be *Strongbow*...

Orchards were major investment and also an insurance policy against lean times. Apple bread and apple cake are as old as the hills, and even some recipes for simnel cake, to be eaten at Easter, include dried apple as well as marzipan, sultanas and raisins. Apples that keep till Easter through Lent are much prized. And so the process that starts with Eve in the Garden of Eden, works its way through black dogs, shot guns, toast, robins, wren boys, tom tits, the wassailing hullabaloo on Twelfth Night and ends with Lent, Hunger, Crucifixion and Resurrection. To be followed of course by the whole business of May Queens, blossom and confetti, fertility and abundance, marriage and initiation, the planting of an orchard, new grafts from old families. In some parts the new bride would go to her new husband's farm clutching the grafts for the new orchard, and these were highly prized, in the same way that coppices were often held by women as land for dowries. The need to improve and keep improving orchards was a necessity, and certain trees were guarded with great pride and even secrecy. They were the investment, the future.

But orchards have another function apart from providing safe courting grounds near to home. Here you can also graze your sheep, which means the land is doubly productive. There is nothing better than to see a flock of good ewes with lambs at foot beneath the May apple blossom, a sight which will stop even the hairiest of men in their tracks. Maybe the Japanese have got a point when they all take a holiday to see the blossom; maybe they are celebrating something of the delicateness and transient beauty of being alive, which we have all but lost.

Cider however was not just the drink of the working man, it was drunk with pride on the tables of large houses and was regarded in some cases as superior to claret and canary wine, which may not have travelled that well in the past. Even as recently as the last war, cider was served on the high tables of Oxford Colleges, for lunch. Possibly the 'Occupation' of France at the time had something to do with it or maybe the Germans were really only after the Calvados, and only succeeded on reaching the Pays d'Auge on the third attempt. Wars on the continent have always made good wine expensive or even unobtainable, but Britain has always been able to fall back on its orchards in times of need.

Cider has a long and dignified history and its uses are as much medicinal as for pleasure. No doubt in the lean periods, in the hungry gap of lent, cider enabled the medieval peasant to survive the winter better and must have helped to prevent malnutrition, which is maybe why it was held in such high regard. Indeed it could also be argued that its use on board ships to prevent scurvy not only greatly enhanced the capabilities of seamen and fishermen who undertook long voyages, but enabled them to discover and even settle new lands across the Atlantic.

In 1620, the same year as the Mayflower set sail from Plymouth to America, another lesser known group under Richard Whitbourne set sail from Exmouth, for New-Found-Land and took with them large quantities of Sider, to help make a new settlement which was already being exploited for its rich fishing grounds. The cider was as much for use ashore as afloat. Indeed salt cod was much in demand and an easy source of protein. The rewards were high, but so were the risks. It seems that instinctively they took cider which had high Vitamin C content, and the stronger it was, the better it kept.

In those days production of good cyder was taken far more seriously. For instance in the 17th and 18th century, great debates were instigated about various types of fermentation, which yeast to use, which subtle peculiarities of soil, climate and good husbandry made the best cider, which varieties were best suited to which counties. Treatises were written and papers read to the Royal Society. Grafting and hybridisation were conducted in secret, experiments in what we would call genetic engineering were conducted with the same degree of commitment as if it were a nuclear arms race.

But cider is more than just farm produce. In the West Country good stories are, however, prized as much as the cider itself but the old cider houses or cider clubs are now a rarity. It was here that stories were enriched and embellished, business was done, and in some areas these had the status of a village parliament. Good years and bad years were debated. The 'goings on' of Captain Swing and the plight of the Tolpuddle Martyrs were no doubt much discussed, as was the ensuing battle over the vote, which eventually led to improved wages and the franchise of the farm worker in third Reform Bill of 1884. Industrial workers had incidentally got the vote in 1867. These cider houses varied, some were like pubs but others were either sheds or barns filled with tatty armchairs or the sitting rooms or even farm kitchens. I remember one at Nempnet Thrubwell run by two old ladies, and very popular it was too. There was no sign up or anything, you just knocked on the back door. They were direct links with the land without any interfering middlemen or health inspectors, or personnel in suits carrying briefcases full of regulations.

The demise of the cider house is partly due to the licensing laws, for at one time cider was in the same bracket as sweets and ginger beer, and taxed accordingly. It was a farm product like eggs and bacon. But the real problem was not just decimalisation but the fact that anyone producing over 1500 gallons was deeply scrutinised, and most farmers have an aversion to being deeply scrutinised.

Also there was a perception problem. The image of cider was as a cheap alternative to beer or spirits, it was the drink for alcoholics and teenagers. The drink for naive tourists who only wanted rough old stuff you could take home and impress your mates with, using such names as *Dead Dog Cider* and *Drowned Rat*. Indeed tourists are so gullible that they believe the rougher the cider is, often the better it must be and even pay more for rough stuff. Cider is often a pound or more a gallon in Devon than it is in Somerset. Technically *scrumpy* is a term used for cider that has other fruit and even beet root shoved in it to give it colour. Curiously enough the word *scrumpy* is lacking from the 1933 Shorter *OED*, though *scrumping* is a term long in use for stealing apples. Nostalgia and childhood holidays in the West Country would not be the same without cider, or *Rosie* for that matter.

But the perception problem does not end there. Young farmers, whose grandfathers only bought farms because of the quality of the orchards, now go away to college and learn all about tractors, pesticides, profit and loss. They drink lager, a German concoction which I believe is still popular with football hooligans. Television and cheap foreign holidays also have a lot to answer for. Few if any of these young farmers have I suspect replanted orchards. The temptation is to knock over the last few trees nudge them with the front end loader and then whack in a crop of maize or corn, when father isn't looking.

One of the saddest sights I have ever seen was on a back lane near Allowenshay where an orchard of ninety acres in its prime, at 25 years old, was bulldozed and grubbed out and the stumps burnt. I would pass it every day on the way to work and the apples were still on the trees. The next year,

1990, was a bumper crop, and we had to do seven weeks of night shift pressing to get 'on top of it'. But these were in the main *Bulmer's Norman* and a part of the Showerings enterprise, which was being shed, as were the grafters. As they say an *accountancy decision*. The land had reverted to the local farmer's son and he was soon growing corn and now maize.

I can still visualise the piles of stumps smouldering in the evening light as I returned home. A friend of mine rescued some of the trunks and they were fine specimens straight and clean as a whistle. It seemed strange that you could get a preservation order for a single tree but a farmer could rip out the largest orchard in the county without even asking permission.

Sadly this has happened all too often, mainly for economic reasons. Even now as I pass the apple loading station, I remember the orchard, but economics are economics and farmers were getting £90 a ton back in the 1970's for cider apples, and it hasn't gone up at all since then. Devon, the neighbouring county, also much associated with cider, has lost 95% of its orchards since the end of the war, a staggering statistic when you think of the size of Devon. It is said that the American forces lost more soldiers to cider and local girls than on the beaches of Normandy. But then Europe, concentrating on production targets and the cult of the *Golden Delicious*, hasn't helped either.

The other end of the perception problem is the fizzy ciders made on the whole from apple concentrate shipped in from Europe or is it China now ? This is brown treacly stuff, caramelised, vacuum sucked, boiled, mistreated in every conceivable way. It is a wonder it ever ferments at all, sugars are no doubt added, particularly for the new yuppy brands with designer names like *Red Mountain, Diamond Thunder Cloud* and the lesser known *Black Zit*. The fizzy cider may satisfy palates in the suburbs and the night-clubs of sleazeland, but it bears no relation to high quality farmhouse cider that is made from cider apples. Strange but true, most of the 'new' ciders have never seen a cider orchard let alone Somerset, Devon or Herefordshire. With global warming we shall no doubt get orchards in Greenland and South Georgia. With so few real cidermakers left, the future is appalling.

In the past, what orchards provided was visible stability. a significant investment, a long term view of farming and the productivity of the land. Great care was needed in planting an orchard, in selecting the varieties needed to help cross pollinate the others, each cropping at a slightly different time of year. And then there are the '*bitter sweets*' and the '*bitter sharps*' with such wonderful names as Slack-me-Girdle, Foxwhelp, Red Streak, Stoke Red, Bloody Turk, Kingston Black, Yarlington Mill, Michelin, Dabinett, Tom Putt, Morgan Sweet, Harry Masters Jersey, Lambrook Pippin, Stembridge Jersey, Brown Snout, Taylors, Sweet Coppin, Chisel Jersey, Tremlett's Bitter, Porter's Perfection and Royal Somerset to name but a few. There are hundreds more... Each with an interesting history all of their own. No doubt one day in Devon there will be a *Ted Hughes*. Like poets each name has its own landscape and following, its own locality its own distinctiveness. These varieties are genetic material we tamper with at our peril. The tragedy may be that some have slipped away in the last fifty years, unsung, unnamed and unnoticed. When you buy cider from the farm, you are buying it straight from source, the apples will have only travelled the length of the orchard, and then a matter of yards into the barn.

You are coming to it, and you are coming to it freshly, and that is important. The link is direct and you are in a sense buying into the landscape, you are keeping it alive, and perhaps more importantly you are taking away with you a drink of quiet complexity and hidden strength that has all the elements of the orchard bound up in it. A powerful fragrance that refreshes you in the heat. To our forefathers sweating it out in the great scything gangs that once mowed our long fields of hay and corn, or later in the year at thrashing time, it must, not just have seemed a miracle, but a necessity.

But orchards once cut down are usually gone forever, and are only commemorated on some street name or *cul de sac* such as *Orchard Close* or *Orchard Drive,* whereas in fact it should be No1 *The Decimated Orchard*, or No 2 *The Tarmac Drive...* A county without orchards is like a kitchen without a larder, a town without a dress shop, a sitting room without a painting, a young girl without an admirer. Cider *is* Somerset and the fruits of many centuries of experimentation lie in the orchards. To smell a cider house whilst the apples are being pressed, is one of the most unforgettable smells you will ever experience, such fragrance that sets your head reeling before you ever taste a drop.

Cider: the forgotten miracle is an introduction to the subject and also an accumulation of stories and anecdotes about the history of cider that I have gathered over the last 20 years, and more particularly whilst working at Burrow Hill, during cidermaking each autumn. To share a small glass or two of mulled cider between friends on a long winter's evening beside the fire, is to partake in one of life's more interesting mysteries. It is after all the indigenous national drink of the Westcountry. You are communing with the Apple God, a mellow and powerful invocation, not only of the orchard, but of the very English landscape that has produced it.

And then there is distilling, but that's another story...

Advice to those who are about to undertake a Sea Voyage...

If you are ever tempted to eat salt beef, which is often very good, you will find that cyder is the best liquor to quench the thirst generally caused by salt meat or salt fish.

Benjamin Franklin   1706-1790

Stay with me flagons; comfort me with apples.

The Song of Solomon II.5

Part One

The Important Thing - Getting To Work

When you go to work at the cider farm, the main thing to do is to take enough clothing, for it can be pretty nippy on a winter's morning, as well as wellingtons, packed lunch and a woolly hat to stop the apple juice getting in your hair or down the back of your neck. The drive to work is the best part of the day, because you can listen to classical music on the radio as you pass through some of the most interesting lanes in Somerset. Being slightly nomadic I tend to live in two places and each journey has its delights. Firstly from the Axe valley, where I have lived for a dozen years or more, there is a three mile lane with stunning views over into West Dorset, real hill-billy country.

Sometimes the mist just lies in the valley, with the hill tops poking out. Pheasants and partridges abound in certain gateways where they are fed by the keepers, and loiter with intent. The school bus has to be squeezed past and sometimes the keeper himself, who looks darkly sideways at anyone with a dog. It always amazes me that people don't pick up more road-kill pheasants and rabbits. Better than being shot at by twelve bores or eaten by the fox. But game is game and technically, so I am told, you cannot pick up pheasants that you have run over yourself, but if you are car number two, that is fine...

The slightly grubby white Renault van starts easily these days but then it is a diesel. It never stays white for long and the back is crammed full of old clothes, jackets, cider, dog biscuits, chainsaws and other useful implements, like felling bars and spanners. The dog, a good looking Springer Spaniel bitch, called Tess, likes to sit up on the passenger seat and cranes her neck forward to spot the aforesaid pheasants and partridges as well as rabbits. Best of all she likes the window down so she can put her head out and her ears fly in the wind... fast roads are boring and only these lanes will do. Keepers look at you even more carefully through even narrower eyes, if you have what looks like a working spaniel...

As the lane rises up out of the valley, you can make out even more of West Dorset, the back end of the hillforts, Pilsdon Pen and Lewesdon Hill, and in the distance, on the skyline, to the east, the radio masts of Rampisham where the World Service does some of its Broadcasting. These masts although ten miles away are a major landmark and I always like to think of all those wonderful languages going out around the globe from that rather inauspicious piece of waste land. Wasteland that is grazed by certain sheep that were once upon a time, in the not too distant past, rustled by a local character in lieu of a debt, and were later found being sold at Exeter market. There are also rumours of it being a secret naval listening station, but you never get to the bottom of these things till years later. Even the series of masts on the Blackdowns, which looked so innocent were linked to GCHQ and were apparently listening to Russian submarine radio traffic. Maybe they have a special frequency for listening in on cider makers... strange things happen in the countryside...

Rampisham, where some years ago the landowner apparently closed the pub down on a whim, because he did not like the traffic congestion, the 'rowdy' behaviour and the noise of people enjoying themselves coming up from the pub garden on a summer's evening. The *'Tigers Head'* was a marvellous pub and the rabbit pie very welcome after a day's shearing, dagging or dipping. Sheep that the landowner in fact partly owned. A strange turn about from the days when overtime and even farm wages were paid in cider.

But then Dorset is Dorset and at times very *Feudal* with it... and there is somehow lingering in certain pockets, this very strange notion that *'you'* actually own the land forever and ever Amen; lock, stock and barrel and everyone who sets foot upon it, or lives in the village, belongs to *'you'* body, purse and soul.

These sorts of feudal attitudes die very hard. Any hint of Socialism or real democracy was seen as a red rag to a Tory Bull, and not a few landowners favoured Moseley's Fascist Party before the war, though they denied it afterwards. One or two were even interned for pro-German views and there were rumours of evergreen swastikas being planted in the beechwoods south of Shaftesbury, that were only visible from the air...

Any criticism of a system which virtually starved farm labourers and forced them to steal firewood or emigrate, falls upon deaf ears. But that's another story and this side of the river is Somerset, well known for its dissent, liberal views and of course the odd rebellion.

The two counties are in some ways like *'Chalk and Cheese'*, an expression which I believe derives from among other things, the natural geography of the neighbouring county to the east, Wiltshire, and the pertinent observations of the much underrated but eminent historian and antiquarian, John Aubrey. He wrote in the 17th century, on all sorts of strange and wandering topics, observing that in the rich, lush, easy flowing cheese land :

" they feed chiefly on milke meates which cooles their braines too much, and hurts their inventions. These circumstances make them melancholy, contemplative and malicious; by consequence whereof come more law suites out of North Wilts, at least double to the southern part. And by that same reason they are more apt to be fanatiques... "

And that on the High Chalk Downlands, where flints, corn and sharp winds abound :

"where tis all upon tillage, and where the shepherds labour hard, their flesh is hard, their bodies strong ; being weary after hard labour, they have not the leisure to read and contemplate of religion but goe to bed to their rest, to rise betime the next morning to their labour."

For a modern and sympathetic appraisal of John Aubrey, his writings, his observation on ancient customs and appraisal of archeological sites, it is worth reading the essay about his life written by John Fowles, recently re-published in *Wormholes*.

Landscape, language and agriculture so closely fitting, so apt and keenly observed... always I try to read the landscape and see where the *chalk* meets the *cheese*. And don't forget that Somerset has given the world that most ubiquitous of cheeses, Cheddar, much imitated, good for shoving in the pocket, but best matured two years or even smoked. Often part of a truckle would lurk in the back of my own van for emergencies... and to be discovered a year later, none the worse for wear or chainsaw oil.

The lane continues intermittently lined with oak and ash. On one occasion many years ago I took some magic mushrooms and drove back down this road in a violent storm. These trees took on weird moving shapes in rainbow colours, as if their arms were flailing, the tree spirits come alive, a memorable and truly extraordinary experience. Ann, the old shepherdess who was with us, also took some mushrooms as well and when we returned home she spent half an hour looking at an old Persian carpet of mine which I had bought in Kashmir. When she came to, she simply said, "James, I had no idea this carpet was so interesting," and with a twinkle in her eye clasped her hands together and raised them in the air, a gesture she had learnt whilst living in the hills during the Spanish Civil War... Her mother had been born at sea round Cape Horn and only had a longitude and latitude in her passport, her father and grandfather ran a handful of sailing vessels trading *guano* from Valparaiso to the Argentine and up to New York... But Ann liked cider and sheep, they had, she said, an affinity for one another. Sadly she died last year, so I always view these trees with a degree of affection and even superstition every time I pass.

Significantly to the left of the lane, on a ridge known as Windwhistle, appears a magnificent line of beech trees reminiscent almost of Buckinghamshire, betraying the chalk cap which lies underneath... to the right, a series of dairy farms that just by chance make among other things Cheddar cheese. So even on this journey to work within a few miles both are evident... and the shepherds I know well up here, and have worked with often, are thin, wiry and very hard-working.

At the top of the long lane is another world, a fast road, a main road, a coaching road, the A30 which I am told goes all the way to a place called London, which I believe is a small settlement beyond Salisbury, some call it the *Smoke*, though other people reliably inform me that it is sandwiched between two cricket teams called Surrey and Essex. That it exists I do not doubt for its people come down here in smart four wheel drive vehicles and go for walks in clean clothes, but where they work they must be packed in very tightly, like chickens in a coop, and as a consequence talk fast and sharp in an effort to be heard above the traffic and each other. Its a miracle anyone survives up there at all... but they do. Some even imagine that they run the country side, but the countryside tends to run itself. Behaviour in the Houses of Common sometimes runs a close second to badger baiting I am told, and anyway if nearly all the common land has been enclosed, surely it should be called the House of Enclosures, or is it Disclosures ?

At the 'T' junction you turn right. There is a quick glimpse over the Vale of Taunton out over the Quantocks so beloved by Wordsworth and Coleridge. And further to the West, the Brendons and even the edge of Exmoor on a fine day, that fine distant blue haze which speaks of heather and rich honey.

Just beyond the junction on the left, there is a sawmill. In fact there are two sawmills here, as well as an old lime kiln, for this is a chalk ridge and the lime was much in demand. One sawmill which belongs to a tree surgeon called Andrew Hutchings. He only works it on Fridays, but I have had some excellent oak from him which he sawed up into sufficient lengths to make a four poster bed. The tractor which he bump started to run the saw bench, had a wren's nest just behind the radiator and the wren didn't seem to mind at all, and returned to her nest after the saw bench had finished its work. Once when Andrew was going on holiday, he even took the tractor back home, a distance of about four miles, and only afterwards realised that he had four small passengers in the nest, so he took the tractor all the way back up the hill again for feeding time... The wren, most sacred of Celtic birds, hunted on Christmas day and killed, then given a royal funeral, and until recently on the flip side of that small but much missed coin, the farthing.

The oak had wonderful ripples and 'burr' effects in it. The smell of the fresh cut oak, the tannin, is incomparable on a fine morning and Bernie White, the carpenter from Hardington who was with me, chose well. His father had been the carpenter before him and he told me you always knew when somebody had died, because you could hear the old saw bench start up to cut some coffin boards into shape. A strange singing noise that has a distinct zing at the end, a bit like sharpening the old reaper but faster.

Next left, down the hill arched over with trees, then there is a fairly fast stretch of road looking towards Ilminster and Dowlish Wake, once the family home of James Hanning Speke, the discoverer of the source of the Nile. No doubt Egypt, Sudan and Uganda, were a far cry from the quiet secluded thatched houses, but a resting place all the same. A bit tame perhaps after all that excitement in Africa, but there is a wildlife park over the hill... Sadly, John Hanning Speke died in a shooting accident. There was, if I remember rightly, some controversy about the source. At the other end of the village is Perry's Cider farm, the second source of the Nile, which still produces good quality farm cider and was patronised by Lord Beaverbrook among others. It also has a small and interesting museum... But the farm which I am aiming for, Burrow Hill at Kingsbury Episcopi, is a little further away, and so I only catch a glimpse of Dowlish Wake, on the port bow, as I pass, through it is close to Allowenshay.

To starboard, the old Poulett estate. Lord Poulett whose family had made their money on brick and tile yards in Bridgwater. In 1849, the sixth Earl married a pilot's daughter he had met at Dublin races and then separated when it was discovered that she was already pregnant by an army captain. The last in line I was told married a barmaid from Blackpool, but sadly he died without an heir. The estate was wound up in 1968 and sold off in small portions to make several farms. Here they had some of the largest specimen trees in the country, 100 ft cherries, silver fir, oaks and ash to fill a ridge. Everything else was taken out and replanted with the ubiquitous softwoods, Douglas Fir and Japanese larch, which tended to corkscrew because the

winters were not hard enough. The outside wall still remains as do the gate houses and a sign which says *STRICTLY PRIVATE* and looks out onto wonderful parkland. Often at other times of the year I would work in the woods thinning larch and sycamore and was once caught out in one of those *'hurricanes'* and I had to run the gauntlet of trees and branches coming down... an interesting experience.

At the large chestnut beside one of these gatehouses, I turn right down a lane which becomes for nearly half a mile a tunnel. The banks are very steep sometimes twenty or more feet high and overhung with hazel, sycamore and ash. You have to be careful because the lane is so narrow that two vehicles can only just pass at the passing places. Real bandit country and excellent for an ambush. In winter the leaves and mud make it very slippery so proceed with caution. Then you enter the famous hamlet of Dinnington, whose importance now lies in the hands of a certain pub called *The Rose and Crown* otherwise known as *'The Dinnington Docks'*, one of the most celebrated pubs in Somerset, known for its eccentric landlord and highly amusing clientele. They even have a fictitious railway and canal with its own Historical Society, which has uncovered such gems as the fact that Queen Victoria's wedding ring was made from the last English gold found in Allowenshay, it must have come out of one of those sandy banks when it collapsed after rain... A special type of very fine clay was dug up here in the 17th century and sent to France for powdering their wigs and of course the mythical battle of Badon was fought here close to the pub, so that they could get ample refreshment afterwards. Sadly the marshalling yards of the railways were destroyed in a Zeppelin raid in 1918, but the turning circle for the barges still floods across the road to this day. As a token gesture to the possibility of flooding, global warming and a sudden rise in sea level around opening time, a lifebelt and various assorted mooring bouys are anchored outside the pub on the wall, just in case...

Then there is a Mayor of Dinnington who once a year at Gala Day wears a gold chain of chocolate money as badge of office. This is also the home of the notorious *Green Arrows* who specialise in the art of formation lawnmower cutting. It is here that we have the annual Christmas, end of season cider-makers meal and session. A sometimes riotous evening which rounds off all those long hard days. A kind of mid-winter Celtic festival in miniature, and if not Celtic certainly pre-Christian.

Past the pub is a fine old gnarled copper beech on the left and then the sewage works on the right. This section also gets flooded quite often. Once in Lopen you are into steep bank territory again. Here another orchard was grubbed out two years ago, but this time a dessert orchard at a place aptly named Snapant. Over the old '303', which I am told also goes to that place called London and then the landscape changes to a fruit growing, vegetable growing, potato growing landscape, almost with a whiff of France, tall slender windbreak hedges of poplar that rattle in the wind and ought to be painted by schizophrenic tubercular artists. Grade one ground, high in fertility and profit.

Then over the new '303' which definitely goes to London, though some also say it goes to Exeter as well. Manic lines of traffic, lemmings on four wheels and something called 'jewel' carriageway. Then, that over with, AND FAR MORE IMPORTANT, first glimpse of the cider farm, one tree, a sycamore on a distant hillock, a homing beacon for thirsty men, that at Christmas time is lit up with fairy lights, run off a small generator.

More lanes and more fields, fields of broad beans, leeks, old tomato houses, onions, carrots, blackcurrants, raspberries, cabbages and turnips. West Lambrook, then a side lane with a glimpse of the *'cider'* monument which has an interesting history. At one point in 1763, the cider tax, which had originally been introduced 120 years earlier during the Civil War, was increased dramatically to pay for the Seven Years War retrospectively, a increase in duty of 4/- a hogshead to 10/- which was bitterly resented by the farmers.

This measure had been brought in by Lord Bute's government and with it the right for Excise men to enter any man's premises to search for cider, which was seen by many, and William Pitt the elder, in particular, as an infringement of human rights and the individual. It was in his campaign to get the increase lifted, that he coined the phrase *'An Englishman's home is his castle'*, a sentiment which brought him much support throughout the West country. So much did it mean to them, that Pitt was rewarded by an eccentric landowner, Sir William Pynsent, who had no heirs, and had, it is said, been suspected of incest with his daughter. He left Pitt a substantial house and farm just outside Curry Rivel at Burton which to this day is known as Burton Pynsent... Of the fate of Sir William Pynsent's daughter, history however does not relate, though some might say, quite rightly, that she got a raw deal... but the laws of inheritance were different then.

To mark his gratitude Pitt commissioned Capability Brown to built a monument on the estate, an elegant slender tower, up whose steps a cow is supposed to have climbed in the nineteen-forties. However there was no room for the cow to turn round and so it had to be slaughtered at the top and brought down in pieces. It is still referred to as the cider monument and is a reminder of the paramount importance that cider had in this district. The monument, which is in fact extraordinarily elegant, overlooks the River Parrett and the whole of West Sedgemoor, a good vantage point for lovers, dog walkers and low flying jets.

There is another tall slender monument on the skyline between Somerton and Street of similar proportions and built some forty years later to Samuel Viscount Hood, Admiral of the East Indies. So in Somerset at least, at the end of the 18th century, and at the beginning of the 19th century, cider was on an equal footing with the Royal Navy, the Honourable East India Company and '*goings on*' at sea. Just down the hill is Butleigh Court, the home of Sir Robert Neville Grenville who experimented greatly with cider and cajoled government, until in 1903 they set up what later became known as the Long Ashton National Institute for Cider Research outside Bristol, a marvellous institution that now has sadly lost most of its funding.

Sometimes you can see flooding around Isle Brewers and this gives you some warning of floods at Midelney and Langport. Indeed if I come the other way across the levels from Somerton, flooding can be a major problem, in bad weather, as the rivers burst their banks and the villages revert to being islands again...

It was after all, in one of these island refuges that Alfred is supposed to have master-minded his guerrilla campaign against the Danes. He later founded an Abbey at Athelney, Isle of the Athelings or Princes. Unfortunately the bakery doesn't survive but there is a rival establishment in Glastonbury called *Burns the Bread*, no doubt run by one of his Scottish poetic descendants. Rumour also has it, that when the odd Viking army appeared at the river's mouth, down at Combwich, the people of Somerset, no doubt fired up on cider, drove them off and slaughtered the rest with gusto. Thank God its only cricket these days. But it is interesting to note that some of the moors were only drained as late as 1830 and the river, tidal to Langport.

As I get near the cider farm, the orchards become more apparent, and the wayside trees have a preponderance of mistletoe, that most ancient of vegetation which has myth in its palm. And very often, in these parts, it is mistletoe which is growing in apple trees, and it is mistletoe which comes into the ciderhouse at the end of pressing in abundance. In some ways the oak, the apple and mistletoe are the sacred trinity, representing strength, fertility and kingship. A point not lost on Sir James Fraser when he wrote *The Golden Bough*, bringing in as he did Zeus, Balder, Celts and Druids.

But in fact, in the West of England, the apple tree should be *The Golden Bough*, heavily laden as it is with rich fruit in autumn, the time of regeneration... A real shame that Sir James did not do what Cecil Sharp did, which is to take an interest in the songs and customs of Somerset... for just across the moor from the Burrow Hill Cider farm and clearly visible is the village of Hambridge. And here it was in Sept. 1903 that Cecil Sharp heard John England the gardener, singing '*The Seeds of Love*', in the rectory Garden, and so impressed was Cecil Sharp by the voice, and the song and the tradition, that he started there and then on his career of collecting folk songs. What people do not know so readily, is that the second song he collected was in the next village of Drayton and this was the Drayton Wassail song which was far more ancient... Indeed 150 years ago Wassail songs were sung throughout the South west on Twelfth night, a custom which is still in place in some villages... and is in effect an ancient relic of a tree-worshipping and cider-worshipping community... In fact the words *Wassail* and *Cider* do not even appear in the index of the shorter version of *The Golden Bough*, which is a shame as they conjure up in all their variety, many of the elements which Sir James would have recognised. Offerings of toast and cider to boys in the tree tops representing the tree spirit, mentions of robins and tom tits and in Ireland, wrens the worshipping of the trees, the encouraging of them to bear fruit, the cajoling of those that do not, the offering of cider and spirit to the tree, the oldest and best in the orchard, the reverence and respect, the need for the whole village or clan to be there, and feeling of certainty that if someone is absent the orchard will not bear fruit or they themselves will not prosper beliefs which are not entirely absent today.

Indeed communion with the apple trees, the awakening of the tree spirit and the banishment of evil spirits, is as important as the sampling of the cider itself. A detailed inspection of all available accounts of the Wassail songs might just yield something very interesting... take this one for instance from John Aubrey again :

"The ploughman have their Twelve- cake, and they go into the Oxhouse to the Oxen with the Wassell-bowl and drink to the ox with crumpled horn, that treads out the corn; they have an old concerved rhythme: and afterwards they goe with their Wassell bowle into the orchard and goe about the trees to blesse them, and putt a piece of toast upon the roots."

This was published in 1686 and the rhyme was ancient then. What is interesting is that the oxen are revered, as it was the oxen that did the ploughing and general cart work on the farm, without which there would be no wheat or barley for bread and feedstuffs... Also the horn of the oxen was crumpled, which meant in those days inward turning, ie it was a good horn shape and not straight... horns were useful as this small excerpt collected as late as 1980, nearly three hundred years later shows :

"the harvest horn was filled with cider and one end stopped with a cork, and carried to the harvest field, passed round and when emptied the horn was blown as a signal to begin harvesting... if the horn was not oiled with cider it would lose its note."

This was collected by Walter Minchinton a Professor of Economic History at Exeter University, from an acquaintance Lionel Walrond. The importance of cider as ritual may well be perceived through these two short but important extracts, an importance which did not vanish with the advent of tea and thermoses :

" Tea was provided at harvest, but they always took cider afterwards. Tea was injurious to health if not washed down..."

Interestingly enough cider tastes wonderful out of small horn beakers which were taken to the fields in pockets and not easily broken, in fact much better than plastic.

In Melbury Osmond, until the late nineteenth century, was the *Ooser*, or *Guiser* a large wooden mask in the shape of a bull's head with opening jaws and horns. Sadly the mask which is probably several hundred years old, has disappeared, and is the only link to a much earlier ritual.

And whilst on the subject of worshipping trees there is always the oak... mighty useful for storing the cider in great vats, and in the construction of barns and barrels. Indeed the location of the oak, and upon which slope it is facing, makes a difference... though new oak barrels are more likely to come from Limousin or from Hungary. Once distillation has been done, the oak gives the cider spirit its colour and the tannins its intricate mellow flavour, mixed in of course with old sherry and whatever else was in the barrel beforehand. What the addition of mistletoe would do, I am not sure, but it would no doubt have some medicinal qualities.

The links with oak and Kings are well known as are the preponderance of pubs called 'The Royal Oak'. Often the old presses were made from oak or elm and lasted as long as 'Men of War' if not longer. The top part of an old press was known as 'summer' and the bottom part 'winter', the two extremes so to speak. Elm was better for the juice and could take long periods of being damp, as well as having an irregular grain which could stand the pressures of cider making.

But enough of this idle musing, turn right at the next 'T' junction up a slight rise beneath *Burrow hill* itself and when you get to the farm a wooden hand and finger points into the yard from a hedgerow with the single word *CIDER*.

This is Pass Vale Farm other wise known as Burrow Hill. The shed is rambling wood and hamstone and covered in green corrugated iron. Once thatched it has the run down appearance which appeals to all and sundry, except for certain health inspectors from supermarkets who turn their noses up at plastic rats, cobwebs, and want everyone to wear food hygiene white hats, frilly aprons and high heels. Official men in suits beware, here be dragons, sheepdogs called *Pirate* and *Badger* and the mercurial owner, Julian Temperley, who apart from producing some of the best cider in the Westcountry, has over the last dozen years, successfully played around with his distillery to great advantage. Accurately described by Frank Browning, a Kentucky apple grower, as *'the brilliant bad boy of English Cider'*.

Julian has taken the Cider bull by the horns and has succesfully navigated his way round and through countless regulations. He has an excellent distillery with miles of copper pipework to show for it. Certainly the cider brandy products are well worth drinking and convey the true measure of the orchard, and the richness of landscape which is that part of Somerset. Down in the 'bond' the cider brandy improves year by year.

With orchards being cut down and the scarcity of middle range producers, it looks as though good cider will, as John Worlidge says in his own introduction, *have to speak for itself*. Julian has a brusque but highly intelligent perception of the cider world. If anyone will keep the ship afloat he will... Also not to be forgotten are Julian Temperley's inevitable choice gems of information, rural spin doctoring, bravado and almost piratical attitude to any regulations and bureaucrats that hinder his experiments in cider diversification. He has had to take on the EEC, the Spanish Government, Customs and Excise, the British Government, various ministers with and without portfolio, the Scots and anyone else who causes paperwork problems.

Usually he wins by a skilfull concoction of wit, cunning and skull duggery, and the bureacrats are sent scuttling back to their desks licking their wounds...

You park your van up, put wellingtons on, gather lunch, smock, dog and clock, make your way across the yard, past the vast piles of apples on the way to the cider house... muttering *'Good Morning'* to whoever you might meet in the yard if they look awake enough to respond.

It is now eight-thirty and the day begins in earnest.

But that which most tempts the Rustick to the propagation of this fruit for the making of this liquor, is, the facile and cheap way of raising and preparing of it... for in such years that Corn is dear, the best cider may be made at a far easier rate than ordinary ale; the thoughts whereof add much to the exhilarating virtue of this Drink, and, I hope will be a good inducement to the farther improvement of it.

John Worlidge 1678

So very good, so fine, so cheap, that we never found fault with the exchange... great quantities of this cider were sent to London.

Daniel Defoe 1726

Part Two

Beer Versus Cider Versus Wine

The strange thing about cider is that until the Second World War, it was made in almost every county of England, as well as parts of Wales, Scotland and Ireland. To be sure there were not always cider apples to hand, but they managed right enough. Ulster for instance has eighty named apple varieties of its own... and lays claim to the earliest apple in Europe, which was found three years ago in a peat bog in Armagh, on the end of a spade, by Dr. Jim Mallory of Queen's University Belfast. It has been dated I believe to around 1000 BC and is, as they say, of normal size, i.e. more likely to be a *cultivar* than a crab... which means that apples have been part of our lives for far longer than we imagine. A Bronze age apple no less, which may mean that the surviving Wassail customs and even the DNA are far more important than we may realise.

According to Peadar MacNeice of the Armagh Orchard Trust it was an offence under Gaelic *Brehon* law to cut down an apple tree, being one of the '*Nobles of the Forest.*' Unauthorised felling was punished by the penalty of forfeiting five cows, a hefty fine even in these days. Imagine cutting down a whole orchard... So cider has a pedigree as long as your arm, and a Celtic one at that...

But its antiquity has not protected farmhouse cider from the ravages of commercial enterprise and the introduction of such things as cheap Dutch gin, smuggled rum and brandy, Scotch whisky, red and white wine, bitter, mild, stout, lager, ginger beer, Vodka, lemonade, even Tequila, to name but a few. Man's ingenuity in extracting alcohol from nature's bounty has fuelled more research than almost any other scientific enterprise on this planet. The heyday for cider was undoubtedly in the late 17th Cent and early 18th Cent. It suffered a dip because of the lead poisoning, around the 1760's, notably in Devon and the importation of cheaper wines from the continent. The fashion of making good strong up-market cider slowly died out. It was squeezed mercilessly by wine from above and beer from below. Today the niche for good quality farm cider is still quite small, rather like real ales were thirty years ago...

But at the end of the 19th century as the farm cider began to rise again in popularity, so the smaller cider factories sprung up and these in turn led to the big industrial cider makers like *Bulmers, Taunton Cider, Showerings, Whiteways, Coates* and *Gaymers*. Amazingly not a few Cider companies ended up being owned by breweries and this continues even today, where the drive for mass markets, I suspect, leads to a diminution of quality and the mass importation of foreign apple concentrate which has kept the price of good cider apples down and resulted in orchards being either not tended or deliberately grubbed out. On a recent television documentary made for *Westcountry*, not one of the 'Big Boys' would admit to the exact percentage of cider apples used in their brews even though they *knew the formula*. Perhaps this is the price of cider going global, but even as this book is going to press, *Mathew Clark* of Shepton Mallet have just announced that they are going to plant another 1,000 acres of cider orchard, which can only be good news.

Unfortunately very few people these days know what real good farmhouse cider tastes like, so in a sense, the general public is at a major disadvantage, but various producers are now bottling cider again, and the re-education about the merits of certain cider apple varieties is well under way. Compare wine, which is nearly always made from one grape variety, to cider which may have a dozen different cider apples in it which makes a much more complex and interesting drink. Perhaps slightly more unpredictable but it makes tastings far more fun. Cider in fact fills the gap between wine and beer very nicely, and always has done.

Uniformity is the death knell of civilisation, as we know it, and yet 'market forces' dictate our lives without us having a real say... Indeed another potent market force is the undeniable pressure of the breweries and their policies of 'tied' houses and monopoly tactics and this has been a potent force in the history of cider. Compared even to HP Bulmer, the brewers were very big barons in comparison. When brewers built their breweries in the last century, they built them like castles, with studded gates, towers, high walls, even battlements. In fact they were more like prisons or naval dockyards, and they had good reason to be. Mob rule in times of unrest, famine or political movements always had a good go at getting free beer. What better target than the local brewery which symbolised the tyranny, not only of alcohol but of an industry where profiteering off the backs of the working classes had an obvious and visible link. Beer was their escape valve and often the pay packet was a good deal lighter when it hit the kitchen table on Friday night or more often than not Saturday morning. For a mob to break into your brewery must in a sense have been a back-handed compliment.

Bitter battles were fought not just with police but with troops and temperance *wallahs* and even clergymen. Drunkenness was fine round a 'posh' dinner table or in an officer's mess but out in the streets, it was social disorder, unlawful anarchy and above all unchristian, even pagan, and thus the legitimate target for Temperance Societies, reformers and clergymen wishing to steal the one perk the working class had inherited, the right to get sozzled. The inclusion of 'husbandry' in the Truck act of 1887 meant that cider could not be legally given as part of farm wages, though most farmers chose to ignore this and farmworkers preferred the cider so long as it was drinkable and the farmer fair in his treatment of them...

What it meant in practice however was that farmworkers and perhaps more particularly the industrial workers were paid cash on Friday nights and the weekend binge became a celebration of that right, whereas the old system allowed men on farms about four pints a day over the week which was better for their health and for family economics.

An interesting note comes from AK Hamilton Jenkin the social historian whose books on Cornwall deserve a far wider audience. His words could have applied to anywhere in the south west :

"The gentry... though they were quick to complain of the debauchery of the labouring classes when it resulted in any interference in the daily routine of their work, they made little attempt either to check the smuggling trade or to regulate the iniquitous 'cider allowance', which to a certain extent in Cornwall, and to a large extent in Devonshire, was forced upon the agricultural labourer in part payment of his wages...

Further more these same gentry, however much they might censure the intemperance of the poor, were nothing loath at election times to connive at the methods of their chosen candidates for Cornwall's 'rotten' boroughs who found the provision of quantities of strong liquor a cheap and effectual means of buying the support of the poorer voters."

Accurate information about cider drinking is difficult to get, but the prodigious quantities reputed to have been drunk were often *ciderkin*, the watered down second pressing of cider, rather like small beer for the haymaking and harvest where men would sweat it out fairly quickly... cider could often be twice the strength of beer, so even watered down it had a fair kick...

Some information comes from two reports by the Poor Law Commission into the Conditions of Women and Children in Agriculture. One in 1843 and the other in 1867. These Surveys were conducted in Somerset, Devon, Dorset and Wiltshire. A few extracts give the general picture :

"In the cider counties part of the wages of women is paid in cider; this is also the case with the wages of men, and also boys from the earliest ages at which they begin to work. A man has three of four pints of cider a day, a woman half that quantity. The man's cider is reckoned worth from 1s.3d. to 1s.6d. a week."

Mr A Austin

Interestingly enough women's wages were varied and depended on the job in hand, but all had cider attached.

In Devonshire women's wages are listed as follows :
*Stone-picking 1d. a seam (2 barrowfulls)
or 1s a-day with cider
Apple-picking 7d. a-day with one quart of cider
Potato-digging 1s a-day with one quart of cider
Clover-picking 8d a-day with cider
Hay-making 8d a day with cider
Harvest 10d a-day with cider*

Mrs Cozens 1843

How many people would work like that today I wonder, but women always seemed to get half what men earned which wasn't really fair, but then they tended to work a shorter day and although the work may have been very monotonous it was perhaps not as hard as men's work.

Two other quotes from Devon :

"Women always get half men's wages; they get in general 8d a-day and cider."
George Moxey

"I give 7d a day to women with a basin of broth at their dinner or one pint of cider, which makes it up to 8d."
Mr Huxtable.

But then the women didn't always get the cider to drink :

"The cider received by the women in part of their wages is not commonly drunk by them; it is more frequently kept for their husbands, though there are cases where it is partly, or even wholly consumed by the women themselves."
Mr A Austin 1843

A raw deal, but then about this sort of the cider itself, few were ever complimentary. It was an acquired taste and dry cider, sharp as a rusty scythe that's just taken an edge. You were always supposed to hang the scythe in an old apple tree, another link with corn and apple, the superstitions interlinked. But about the cider some of those who did not have to do the work regarded it as a kind of lethargic drug, and in a sense they had a point agreed by two very differing gentlemen...

"The liquor refreshes and stimulates him, (the farm labourer) but wears him out, for common cider is not nourishing but exciting, like spirit and water. West Country labourers will never be what they might as long as this system goes on."
Sir Thomas Dyke Acland

*" An' whet do 'em gi' ?
Zour Zider an cheese and enuff to chuck a dorg."*
George Mitchell c. 1870

George Mitchell, who started life as a stonemason, was a great reformer and campaigned with Joseph Arch for the minimum wage for farm workers and the right to vote. Every year for fourteen years they held meetings on Ham Hill above Montacute, and some gatherings were as large as 20,000. The vote came in 1884 with the third Reform Bill so long as the farm workers were renting a cottage no matter how small the property. For the first time in their history the farm workers had a say in their own political and social situation and in a sense their future. Trade Unions became respectable though they were always seen as a threat to the farmer's well being. Wages slowly increased, though they still remain very low compared with industry even today. As always it came down to economics :

"The labourer in a year takes off his master's hands about two hogsheads of cider and satisfies one his bodily appetites at the cost of 15% of his earnings."

Acland & Sturge 1851

And Mr Austin again :

"The cider which is sold to the labourer by his master, or which is given in lieu of wages, is of an inferior kind, not made for the market but for home consumption. It is represented as strong and rough, qualities prized by those accustomed to drink it. I am however inclined to think that the estimated value between master and labourer is too high."

The last point being very valid and an extra 1/6 a week would have made all the difference. Indeed the perks on a farm were, if added up, often half as much again. It was often the slow withdrawal of perks with enclosure and the fact that wages did not go up which made their lot so bad. Women often took up gloving, buttoning or net making to compensate, and this in the hours after they had worked in the fields or after school.

Some preferred the outdoor life and said it was healthier and in some ways they were probably right. TB, Pneumonia and Cholera were lethal in close packed factory houses. Cider was often the only alleviation to suffering and was consumed on a vast scale.

"Every farm in the cider counties has an orchard and cider is part of the regular annual produce. The best cider is sent to London or elsewhere..."

A Austin 1843

To give some idea of the acreage we are talking about, the following table from 1894 showing the size of cider orchards in the cider counties was as follows may hint at its importance :

Devon	26,000 acres
Hereford	26,000 acres
Somerset	24,000 acres
Worcestershire	20,000 acres
Gloucestershire	18,000 acres
	114,000 acres

Dorset is not included in this assessment but to give some idea, back in 1793, there were according to John Claridge, 10,000 acres of orchard in Dorset, and Dorset was not as large as Devon or Herefordshire by any means.

There was obviously a great distinction between the good cider and the rough cider, in fact a class distinction. It wasn't that there wasn't good cider, it was just that the best cider was saved for the farmer and his friends or sent to the big cities for a fair exchange. There was often what was called *"GOOD ENOUGH CIDER "* i.e. it was just *Good Enough* for the farm workers... Any better and they would not have been given it to drink, any worse and even they would not have drunk it...

Even within the last forty years, one gang of sheep shearers in West Dorset who were partial to a drop of cider, would drive into a farm, test the cider and if it wasn't up to scratch they would drive on out again, their job being hard enough without a reliable supply of good cider. Their assumption being that if the farmer couldn't make good cider his sheep would also be in poor condition...

This also this brings out the point that you can work on cider when beer is often too gassy and not really a thirst quencher when it counts. There is something about apples which still refreshes you more than beer, if you are working outside... Bale humping on a hot day is a job which should qualify for free cider, but then bales have got bigger over the years... Carbonated ciders don't work as well either, though *Babycham* bottles are just the right size for drenching sheep, but then *Babycham* was made from pears and lifted the post rationing spirits of many a young girl in the late fifties and early sixties.

But to return to the farm cider, the working cider, the peasant, cider one observer from Exeter, Prof. Walter Minchinton simply put it like this :

" For much of the history of cider making, there have been complaints about the poor quality of cider produced."

And perhaps the last word on the subject of rough old farm cider should rest with an anonymous Herefordshire farmer from the 1920's :

" I paid 'em to make it, and I paid 'em to drink it and still the beggars aren't happy. So I stopped making it."
Herefordshire farmer c 1920

And this is terribly sad, imagine if the French 100 years ago had started to adulterate and water down their medium quality wines, add sugar, beetroot and turnip,

where would their industry be today ? The tragedy is that cider has gone down the road of industrialisation with the rest of agriculture, but has not fully realised the consequences. It is, as one French cidermaker pointed out, a difference of philosophy, and he has a point.

In complete contrast to the anonymous Herefordshire farmer and at the other end of the scale so to speak, is this wonderful quote from Percy Bulmer the founder of the Bulmer's Empire, in a letter to Sir Edward Elgar in about 1887, and this shows the extent of his vision to re-establish cider as a middle or even upper class drink, as it had been in the eighteenth century... it was and still is a case of perception and quality.

"Cider", he said," no doubt has a future before it and will take its place one day as a great national drink. We have overcome a great many difficulties and hope to work the subject out entirely before very long. Trusting you will have a pleasant winter in the South and will find time to write a cider symphony to encourage this struggling industry..."

Whether Elgar ever wrote a cider symphony is doubtful, but who knows it may yet turn up in someone's pigeon loft...

Bulmers had a good eye for business and publicity opportunities and have bought out many of their rivals. As mentioned above the actual levels of cider apple juice, in some concoctions, is I think open to debate. Labelling is perhaps in need of reform when so much effort is spent 'concentrating' on the foreign market, but then maybe keeping cider alive in whatever form can in a sense be seen as a good thing, even for the smaller producers, who may then attract the more curious and perhaps discerning customers.

But to return to the nineteenth century, the breweries also grew up and came of age in the industrial cities, alongside the factories that supplied their thirsty clients.

Even a few public schools had their own breweries and every boy was given a pint of small beer a day to keep him healthy. The industry required not just intuition, good hops and a fortress, it required good water and management on a vast scale, as well as a distribution network that extended to the North West Frontier of India. Bottled ale travelled well if it did not explode. The industrial revolution which was far more of a social revolution than the French or American revolutions, sucked in vast armies of farm workers who might otherwise have been working on the land, to make among other things farm machinery to reduce their numbers even more. And where did the Captains of Industry move ? they moved to the countryside and farmed, where the air was cleaner, because that's what gentlemen did. It goes on today but the gentleman who pays dearly to shoot the pheasants that haven't been run over on various lanes, or worse still poached, is more likely to have come from the city or chambers, where getting your hands dirty is a rare occurrence indeed. Raising a family on farm worker's wages today is something few would contemplate. Image and reality, as always, are somewhat in conflict.

So in a sense good farmhouse cider has been more or less squeezed out by beer from below and from above in the last thirty years with cheap, but very good foreign wine. The great boom in the wine industry has made England the sorting house of the world. Palates are forever getting more exotic, new world, old world, no doubt the Siberian Chardonnay will soon be on the way, matured with husky breath. Cider is in great danger of being left behind and yet it has, I suspect, a far more interesting and diverse genetic history than a grape or an ear of barley. It is far more complex and in a sense sophisticated process when several apples are working together. When you peer into a cider house, by that I mean the barn where the cider is made and sold, you peer into half darkness that is not just medieval, it is primeval. It has the sanctity of the cave, the air of mystery

of a chapel or crypt, it has the smell and atmosphere of oak, apples and tannin. A headiness, a fermented symphony of subtle tastes and odours, a kind of democracy that predates the feudal age where even the poorest pensioner is treated as a valued customer.

Gossip is paramount for the cider house is the nerve centre of the rural intelligence network, every dirty deed and extra marital fling is scrutinised, every customer vetted and vital information extracted more delicately than a wisdom tooth. Matters of state are discussed and debated over the barrels just as vigorously as they are in Parliament and with far more humour.

And so it is that every autumn, various casual workers descend on the farm and get their hands not just dirty but black with tannin. the tell tale mark of a cider maker building cheeses day in day out, for weeks, even months on end. One of the more famous workers at Julian Temperley's is 'Pigeon Biter' though catching him working is indeed a rare occurrence except stirring it a tea break with a teaspoon... He is called 'Pigeon Biter' because of a habit that gamekeepers have, of biting the back of a pigeon's head to kill it, crushing the skull, but not actually taking the whole head off. A very quick and humane way, and far better than twisting their necks. This was used in pigeon lofts and dovectoes when up a ladder, where space and balance could sometimes be a problem. 'Pigeon Biter', who no doubt, one day, will write his memoirs, is a fund of information when it comes to such subjects as the First World War, current trends in gamekeeping, dog-breeding, wild meat cookery. More to the point, good conversation whilst building cheeses is a vital ingredient of the cider, and no doubt the cider benefits. Intellectual cider is a rare commodity these days and its image has fallen on hard times. Alas farmhouse cider, that most rural of drinks, has become a victim of the industrial revolution and the industrialisation of the countryside. But there is no reason why it shouldn't be ressurected. It was good enough for Charlemagne and it was good enough for John Worlidge, who, in 1678, states that in a certain competition held in London :

"a barrel of Redstreak surpassed the best Spanish and French Wines'."

And the prices paid for good apples then were phenomenal...

"Redstreak apples have been sold after the rate of five and sometimes eight shilling the bushel and the cider made of that fruit sold for eight pounds the hogshead and if two or three years old for twenty pounds, the Hog's head, the same as the best canary."

John Worlidge

An extraordinary fact but apparently true, unless of course it was a publicity stunt... Even Royalty espoused the cause of cider so they were partaking not just in the national drink but in a certain undefinable pride in the landscape which had produced it. Patriotic palates and even a kind of robust rural nationalism were also at work. But the connection between cider and beer, or to be more precise between apples and barley is not lost on John Worlidge who makes this acute observation about rural economics on the ground floor, so to speak...

"But that which most tempts the Rustick to the propagation of this fruit for the making of this liquor, is, the facile and cheap way of raising and preparing of it... for in such years that Corn is dear, the best cider may be made at a far easier rate than ordinary ale; the thoughts whereof add much to the exhilarating virtue of this Drink, and, I hope will be a good inducement to the farther improvement of it."

John Worlidge 1678

These extracts from " VINETUM BRITTANICUM" or a Treatise of CIDER And other wines and drinks extracted from fruits growing in this Kingdom" Printed for Thomas Dring, over and against the Inner-Temple-gate and Thomas Burrell at the Golden ball under St. Dunstan's Church in the Fleet Street 1678. Dedicated to Elias Ashmole Esq FRS who was none other than the man who helped found the Ashmolean Museum in Oxford and was also a good friend of John Aubrey...

The copy of this book, which I borrowed to read in my spare time whilst working at Burrow Hill, belongs to Julian Temperley. The feel of the book is wonderful, the paper the printing , the illustrations, exquisite, the binding in calfskin, the Cider Bible, rewriting Genesis and the Book of Revelations.

As to health John Worlidge also mentions the beneficial side effects of drinking good cider for it induces and enhances vigour as well as longevity, and refers, *'as does my Lord Bacon,'* to a certain Morris team in one of the manors belonging to the Earl of Essex which *'has a joint age of 800 years'*. Between eight of them gives an average of 100 years old and they were as he says *constant* cider drinkers. Not bad for a single village...

Many have sworn that cider and apples have kept them alive longer and it may well be that all this research into preventative medicines will one day tell you that *'an apple a day will keep the doctor away...'* which is something of course you always knew to be right all along...

Cider, like *Guinness*, is good for you. The real problem today is that there just aren't enough high quality cider farms left.

Moreover, cider was such a health giving drink that Englishmen newly prosperous... would be a strong and healthy people, and Long Lived... able to goe forth to *Warre* and bee a terror to all our *Enemies*.

R Austen 1653

Cider... generous, strong, sufficiently heady... excites and cleanses the stomach, strengthens the digestion and infallibly frees the kidney and bladder from breeding the gravel stone...

John Evelyn *Pomona* from *Silva* Royal Society 1664

Redstreak apples have been sold after the rate of five and sometimes eight shilling the bushel, and the cider made of that fruit sold for eight pounds the hogshead, and if two or three years old for twenty pounds, the Hogs head, the same as the best canary.

John Worlidge   1678

Part Three

The Cider House - Burrow Hill

Now to the nitty-gritty, or as you might say the core of the operation, and a visit to the cider house which is the nerve centre for work in the autumn. The cider house is a long rambling barn, divided into three parts. The first part is where the vast barn doors open as if onto a threshing floor which it probably once was. Here lies the old press, so vast that some hardly recognise it for what it is or was. A couple of tall screw threads and a bed six feet by six feet, with a small runnel for the juice. These presses are like elephants and just as valuable. Their size, their solidity, their presence lurks in the barn dark. They speak volumes, they are from the age when cider was king and were as highly prized as 'Men of War'. Greater size means greater pressure, means bigger cheeses means more juice per cheese, means more cider per man per day.

The trick is to press the apples before they get too rotten, and it was always a major job crushing the apples through a mill, mechanical or otherwise. Some of the old farms still have the walk round granite troughs with a roller powered by a horse, otherwise known as *One Horse Power Cider*. These are rare now but well worth keeping an eye open for. Bear in mind the advice given in 1708 about what sort of horse to employ for this rather boring job...

"Be cautious next a proper Steed to find
Whose Prime is past; the vigorous Horse disdains
Such servile Labours; or, if forc'd, forgets
His past Achievements, and victorious Palms
Blind Bayard rather, worn with Work and Years

Shall roll th'unwieldly Stone ; with sober Pace
He'll tread the circling Path till dewy Eve
From early Dayspring, pleas'd to find his Age
Declining, not unuseful to his Lord."

John Phillips

Maybe this advice was meant to be applied to farm labourers as well, who knows... but for the horse it must have been what they call a circular operation. Some troughs are so large that they will grind half a hogshead at a grist, and therefore several hogsheads a day. But these horse troughs are almost unknown in Somerset today, they are more of a Devon, Hereford and Gloucester phenomenon. It may well be that most of Somerset's stone is limestone in one form or another and will react with the cider, in fact the apple juice will probably dissolve it away in time and taint the cider. No doubt also the granite or gritstones were difficult to manhandle once it left the Schooners or the Severn Trows. Other devices have smaller but more efficient apple engines powered by hand or water, and some of these were invented in the 17th century.

John Worlidge himself describes one that will press five to eight bushels an hour and a larger one designed by Mr Henry Allen, a cabinet-maker of Exeter Street, near the Strand made from oak, elm, beech, lignum vitae, brass and iron, which will process 20 hogsheads a day, which is good by any standard. At one time there were plans for devices where apple engines could be placed on rafts or barges and powered either by a river or even the tide, like an undershot mill. There were even proposals for their use on the banks of the Thames, thus enabling cider to be made in the heart of the city. Such was their optimism and ingenuity in the 17th century, and much to be admired.

My brother Roger and I, once bought a small horse drawn cider press from a couple of farmers at Silton on Stour, Eddy Martin and his brother, and with it was an apple engine. Roger rigged it up to a single cylinder Lister diesel engine, but essentially it was no different to Worlidge's Ingenio or Mill and had a stone roller for crushing. The apples went in on top and the pomace came out the bottom and was collected in small half barrel with rope handles, which was then dragged a few feet towards the press. Both the press and the apple engine are now in New Zealand, where they are still used by my brother, who when he is not making cider, binds books and collects old motorbikes.

But I digress... from the dark of Burrow Hill Cider House one's eyes get used to the dim light and you can make out vast regiments of bottles and flagons laid out on trestle tables and upturned barrels. Flagons of cider, bottles of *aperitif*, bottles of *eau de vie*, bottles of apple juice and cider vinegar, stouter darker bottles, of fermented sparkling cider and last but by no means least, bottles of cider brandy, that John Worlidge himself would have been proud of. The ultimate product, the refined essence of apples captured and distilled, the heart of the matter.

Artistic labels jump out at you from every corner. Sheep, orchards, apples, dancing, young lovers, chickens. This is the shop floor. When people come in, they pause and look around in amazement that anything like this should still exist. This is the place of pilgrimage, the Holy Grail, the Golden Fleece, the Garden of Eden on tap. And at prices anyone can afford. £4 a gallon is only 50p a pint... which is a third of what you pay in a public house. A gallon is the same in volume terms as six bottles of wine. The wine is twice as strong, but cider still wins hands down for value.

Its unadulterated, unadorned, and perhaps even underpriced.

The other beverages have to be tasted, tried, swirled round the tongue, absorbed and then knocked back. Each delectable in own way, each dependant on the stills. One still is called *Josephine* because she is large and reliable, and the other is called *Fifi* because she is small and fast. Both were made in Paris raised in Normandy and although showing their age a little, take a shine and can perform magnificently when required. But they live in the next village and will be dealt with later.

The new addition, however, which is proving very popular is the *apple aperitif* which is cider brandy mixed with Kingston Black apple juice and coming out at about 18% a rich round, not too sweet, not too dry, long refreshing burst of apple which will have you singing in the aisles, and is perfectly safe to give your great-grandmother. It is rather like a *Pommeau* in the same way that *Pinot* is derived from Cognac. Portugal of course specialises in port which is why the British army spent so long there during the Peninsular War. Many enduring links were made then and many army officers came back with spaniels as well as medals and pipes of port. A pipe being nothing to do with Scottish regiments but a measure equivalent to two hogsheads or four barrels. A measure the same as a butt. In those days not just liquor would be stored in barrels but, beef, peas, hams, fish, anything that needed protecting from the vagaries of the climate and pilfering hands. Big enough to store a man... which is precisely what they did with Nelson... Pickled him in rum and brought him home, or was it brandy ? *England expects every man to do his dhobi.* Indeed many column inches have been written about him and his exploits with Emma... all that dirty washing in Naples.

Curiously enough, during the Napoleonic wars, the trade embargo and blockade must have increased interest in cider and its offspring immensely. It may well be that the incidence of illegal stills during and after the war led to the strict Scottish regulations that are still in force today. Keeping the Scots whisky under control has always been a problem for the English and for the Scots a game rather like poaching, a source of great delight when they outwit those who live south of the border. One has only to think of *Whisky Galore* and the real life situation posed by the terrible shortages of the necessities of life and a war in Europe which was as remote to those in the Outer Isles as it was to the Eskimos. To ground that particular ship with that particular cargo, which might well have gone straight to the bottom of the Atlantic, in that particular place, in that particular weather, was an act of great compassion to their fellow men. And sure enough as foretold, some of the very same bottles have been unearthed recently and sold at auction. But that is another story...

But any distillery in England has to be in the shadow of the kilt, and there were even in the 1930's a few distilleries that were run on the side in certain outlying islands between Harris and North Uist. Even Dartmoor should produce enough peaty water for a classic malt not unlike Lagavulin... But in Somerset everything has to be squeaky clean. On the *cider brandy* stills there are at least 68 locks and stamped lead seals so that temptation does not get the better of you.

First off the still is the *'eau de vie'*, it is fiery but very full of apple and superb on strawberries and in fruit salad or drunk neat with coffee like *grappa*. It is clear as all spirit is, but has surprising character for such a young spirit. Worlidge describes cider brandy as :

"very excellent, quick and burning."

But the real workhorse is the cider brandy, aged for three, five and ten years, more like a Calvados though different in several ways. The stills are the same, but the apples, the cider and the soils and the climate are different and it does not have that long mustiness that old *Calvados* has, as if it has been lurking in a cellar for twenty years. Here the distinctive aroma of apples is carried over into the distillate and smoothens out in the barrels remarkably quickly. It is high time that the West Country regained its industry back again, for there was a perfectly good industry which was taxed separately from cider, but was forced underground by the legislation already referred to in the 1820's which tightened up on the whisky distillers. Battles with Europe and the EEC and Spain in particular over the use of the term *'Cider Brandy'*, a term that the EEC agreed on ten years ago, have now been won, but the attack was below the belt, and should have logically, if it was going to succeed, have included all the other brandies, cherry, pear, plum, old tractor tyres, ferrets, lurchers, anything else that could be brewed up into a lethal concoction. Just because it didn't wear a kilt doesn't mean that it's illegal.

On the walls of the cider house hang old Acts of Parliament from the reigns of Queen Anne, George I, II and III which outline the cider tax and refer to the fact that cider for distilling should be taxed separately hence implying that distilling took place on a fairly large scale legally, not just in the eighteenth century but well into the nineteenth.

The second part of the cider house is to one side and down a step or two into the darkness. Here are are the long lines of barrels, their taps sticking out into the lime light. It is here that the business is done filling up every sort of container imaginable. There is a distinctive squeak of a new tap every time it is used. These barrels are holding about 100 gallons and started life in Portugal holding port then maybe went north to Scotland and then came south to be flushed out for cider. Old rum casks are much prized and rum cider has its own peculiar but likeable taste for Christmas. Every so often the corks have to be taken out to let 'air in' and the level tested. This also prevents back pressure. Keeping barrels in good condition is a skilled art and they are washed out regularly. Also the main secret is to keep the temperature even. This way the cider keeps longer. This is the powerhouse of the enterprise. It is here that people come and buy the cider, it is here that your reputation is made or lost. It is in the very act of testing and buying the golden liquids that you commune with the Apple God. The cider, the libation, the holy sacrament which in a pub is taken with bread and cheddar cheese topped off with a pickled onion, which may not be the only pickled thing around after a while. In the old days when the men would send in the boy to the barn to fill up the costrel, the small barrel slung from the waist holding about a gallon, some farmers would make him whistle all the time, so that even in the darkness he could not take a glass or two extra. Costrels were the daily ration and carried into the fields and much prized, for obvious reasons.

What is good about cider is its thirst quenching abilities in summer. At one time I would drive round farms and villages where I worked, sharing the odd gallon or two of cider with friends. Ten gallons at shearing time was nothing on one farm near Durweston in Dorset, and there were over 1,000 sheep to shear. Even now I can visualise sitting down on the shearing floor with our backs against the wall, in both senses of the word, cooling our *inventions* and regaining our dignity among the smell of sweat, lanolin and sheep shit. That was always an enjoyable job, but the oil had to be there, otherwise one's throat became parched. You often only needed an odd sip every now and then. With orange squash you drink too much and sweat buckets, and beer doesn't do too well in the gullet when you're bending over all the time. Cider is very much the yardstick, a measure of standing in the community, where quality and quantity combine. Without cider the whole agricultural framework in the West Country would have fallen apart long ago...

On a summer's day imagine that taste of apples hidden in a long golden glass, slipping down, the direct association, the magic of orchards held in your hand. Or else, if the cider is too strong and makes you sleepy, you can mix it in equal parts with lemonade, cut fresh fruit into it, add some mint and you have a *Poorman's Pimms*, and just as refreshing for a tenth the price.

And in winter, when the nights are cold and the east wind is blowing, and you are night-lambing and your hands are frozen, there is nothing to compare with mulled cider, a few spice bags, containing cinnamon, nutmeg, ginger, mace and cloves. The whole essence of the east, sniffed and procured. Add cider, lemon and sugar to a pan that doesn't induce alzheimers... i.e. stainless steel rather than aluminium. Mulled cider, provided it has mulled long enough and hasn't had the alcohol boiled off, is heart warming in a way which beer just isn't. Mulled cider keeps all sorts of things at bay... scurvy, rheumatism, arthritis, TB, pneumonia, diseases of the spleen, kidney stones, trench foot and melancholy.

The only problem which arose from cider, apart from excess, was in the eighteenth century, when a disease called *Devonshire Colic* was diagnosed and cured in the Hot Baths at Bath. Cider makers had inadvertently used lead to line some of their runnels and the cider had absorbed this steadily and rather like Romans using lead acetate to sweeten and preserve their wine, the lead caused a few problems. Amazingly the cure which was prescribed in Bath was simply to sit for six hours a day in the waters and the relative weightlessness induced the lead, which had accumulated in the body, to be to peed out naturally at a much higher rate in the urine. A cure which has only recently been understood working with lead workers at Avonmouth. The doctors charged nothing for their services, only that they could observe the patient's progress. The cost of treatment being the cost of staying in Bath and rendering yourself liable to gaming tables and the pleasures of the town as well as its well-displayed curved beauties in stone and skirt. Needless to say lead is no longer used for any purpose in cider. Copper nails are used in the boards and they are inert. Iron also has to be avoided as this taints the cider. Anything organic however will be gobbled up. In the old days a side of beef, 'rats', 'dogs', even drunken GI's have been tipped in. The blood and protein helps to feed the yeast and get them off to a good start. One farmer had pigeons shitting on his apples in the barn. He shot them, the cider was never the same, the nitrogen had been providing a good kick start. Health, Safety and Supermarkets beware. Good old Somerset customs usually have some foundation in science, like *wassailing* and *dwyle flunking*...

Wassailing is when the old and not so old men of the village sing to the trees, put toast dipped in cider in the branches, shout, beat the trees and awaken the spirit, some with shot guns. In some places it was a male thing and traditionally the women stayed at home and locked the men out till they could guess what was roasting on the spit. It is an ancient libation to the Apple God, usually taking place on Twelfth Night, two weeks after the winter solstice, another dark pagan Celtic ritual which has survived against all the odds, a communion wine blest by silent oaths, and references to the black dog.

Dwyle flunking is an old ritual resuscitated, which requires men and women to circle dance round a hogshead of cider, holding hands, and one of the company who has chosen the short straw, has a rag dipped in cider which is flung at the dancers from a short stick. If it hits one, they drink a pint and take over the stick. If it misses the man or woman in the middle drinks a pint. Progressively the whole thing degenerates as one might expect. Law students at Bristol University are particularly prone to this sort of activity in the summer months... after finals are over.

The third part of the cider house is where the action takes place in the autumn. This where the *cheeses* are built and the two hydraulic presses live. This is the front line, the factory floor. This is where the hard work takes place. This is where goats and sheep, men and boys are sorted out, for it requires not just skill but enormous stamina. This is the bit that people are fascinated by, they come for miles to watch. Maybe it is rare sight to see men working hard physically any more, anyway what may appear to be a 'museum' is the real thing, and it is highly efficient. In fact it is a marvel of human and mechanical engineering.

As the invisible clock strikes eight-thirty, apple pickers gather in the yard, the tractor drivers exchange a few words and then '*rev*' up their steeds and with an empty trailer in tow disappear in a cloud of dust and exhaust fumes down the maze of lanes in search of outlying orchards only to return a few hours later fully laden. Then the '*Gentlemen of the Press*' appear, a motley crew, clutching odd plastic bags and haversacks within which lurks their lunch. The day has begun. The Cider God must be propitiated by sacrifice of long hours and hard physical labour, aching limbs and a damp constitution.

First: Hang up your food bag out of dog's and harm's way on a nail, then find and secure your apron. This reaches down to below your knees and protects your clothing from the juice which turns anything black or rust colour given half a chance. These aprons have to be tied with binder twine round the middle and have a habit of coming undone at tea break. Like everything else on the farm, binder twine is indispensable and in short supply. Only small bales have good twine these days.

Second: rearrange the boards and cloths. These are vital and are used for building the cheese, they give it body.

The cheese by the way is nothing to do with cheese that you eat but is a much older use of the word to signify anything that is wrapped with cheese cloths and pressed. A full fourteen or fifteen layer cheese of apple pomace weighs about three quarters of a ton, with a hundred weight on each layer. The boards are made from ash slats and are about three feet by three feet. The cloths which are these days made of nylon, like tight fish netting, are about six foot by eight foot. There is a stainless steel frame, though until recently this was made of wood, usually elm for its resistance to damp. The ash is chosen because it is very pliable and can stand the pressure inside the press. So you have a set of fifteen boards and fifteen cloths. With two presses there are three sets of each.

Next you need the trolley which in this case is on wheels like a primitive railway. The main part of the trolley above the sub-frame is wooden, and on top of this sits the stainless steel tray in which you build the cheese. It has a lip of about six inches and a hole for a pipe to be fitted, this drains the apple juice whilst the cheese is being made, and another shorter pipe is fitted when the cheese is being pressed. This takes the juice away into the collector tank, from whence it is pumped to distant vats. On the bottom of the trolley lie two old boards which are called bottom boards and they are very important because they lift the first layer up out of its own juice, otherwise it would re-absorb as fast as it was pressed out.

To start building a cheese you need apples, or to be more precise apple pulp, or pomace. Here the farmyard comes into play and endless tractors and trailers tip their mounds of apples, which lie like long barrows with every shade of green, yellow, red, russet almost orange among them. These mounds are hosed in with an enormous hose like a fireman's hose. Apples float as anyone who has tried apple bobbing will know. The apples are power-hosed into a trough which acts like a canal and the apples are then bob along like commuters on the escalator till they reach the wooden pit where the conveyor belt picks them up with wooden paddles. The elevator is a masterpiece of engineering and can easily be overloaded, though certain design features have been improved in the past few years. The man whose job it is to keep the pit full is called the 'Pit Boy'. His job is vital and must be attended to in all weathers. Apples go off and it is essential that apples are pressed in their prime. Not too young and not to old, he has to hose them in, or use a broad broom to sweep them in. Sometimes they roll, sometimes, they don't, it just depends on the size of the apple, its consistency and how much debris is in with the apples. Some farmers send in great clods of earth, grass and leaves, branches, shotgun cartridges, voles, bits of badger, anything which will make up the tonnage on their pay chit but doesn't help make good cider. The 'Pit Boy' also has to log in all arrivals of apples from a pensioner on his or her last legs with half a dozen sacks in their boot, to a twenty ton 'artic' load, and reversing one of those big beasts in the yard can be very interesting. Most of the farmers who bring in the apples are somewhat elderly and love to stop and have chat and a cup of tea, this is the high point of their year and the price of apples is vital to their farm economy.

Some farmers even bring in their own apples to be pressed and have their black plastic containers out the back on a makeshift trailers. One of those black plastics holds over 300 gallons, a year's supply near enough. The last farmer who did that, Frank Yandle came from Devon though he was, as he said, living among 'heathen' in Somerset. He wanted to be buried in his little old grey *Wolsley* with leather seats and have a JCB dig the hole for him in a field when he went. He was ninety when he died. We always used to say that we were glad to see that '*he was still alive*', and he would light a cigar look at us with a twinkle in his eye through the cigar smoke, put both thumbs into his waistcoat pockets and declare that he *were* very glad to see that '*we were still alive*' as well, other wise he'd have to go '*elsewhere*' to get his apples pressed. In the last years of his life he cut down his drinking to four pints a day on 'doctors orders'. He always liked his apples black, almost steaming or as we would say 'heaving'. It never did him any harm that we could see. One black plastic in a poor year and two in a good year and he counted every apple and monitored every drop...

Once the apples are in the pit the elevator comes into play and the apples are unceremoniously take aloft, to the apple mill, where they fall into the hopper and are crushed by a high speed mill with six blades like large razor blades about a foot long, set into a drum. The apples don't stand a chance and they then fall down a chute and as the whole system is counter-balanced, the chute only falls when the weight is about a cwt. The two men who build the cheese stand either side of the trolley and one, whose job it is to pull the chute, pulls it at just the right moment and the apple mush called pomace, is then spread on to the cloth and the cloth folded in with hospital corners. The secret is to get the layer of pomace even, firm and spread as widely as possible. Once the cloth is folded in, and the frame removed, the other person puts another board on top, careful to get it exactly vertical over the last board, and then throws a cloth across the frame which has been put down on it. The cloth is spread out and the process repeated till the cheese is complete, about three foot high and fifteen layers thick...

The cheese is then trundled into the press and the pumps switched on. Belts whirr, wheels turn, the building vibrates.

Water is slowly pumped into the hydraulic ram giving a pressure of about 150 tons. The juice pisses out... a marvellous dramatic moment, which is repeated every twenty minutes or so. Two people can build between three and four cheeses an hour if the apples are flowing well. The whole system with two presses is wonderful, for as one press is going up the other one is going down, and then the old cheese is trundled to the end of the barn where it is unloaded layer by layer. The pomace now squeezed dry like cardboard and is thrown or flicked into a trailer or muck spreader, to be fed to sheep or cattle. No doubt it could be fed to pigs and used to produce Somerset air dried *Palma -*

type ham at a push.

It is a long and at times boring procedure, very repetitive but very necessary. A good team will produce anything up to two thousand gallons day like this in eight hours which in fact is nearer seven hours, as half an hour is spent washing down and clearing up and another half an hour spent in tea breaks. The lunch break of course unpaid and not counted in. Sometimes in years of glut, shift work has had to be introduced from 6 am till 10 pm with the change over at 2 pm. One press was built by *STOWE* of Bristol and the other by *FIELDING & PLATT* of Gloucester, both dating like the stills from the thirties. Massive wonderful bits of heavy engineering with a shiny 'silver' ram that rises majestically and squashes *'the life blood out of the heathen apple'.* The sight of the cheese dripping, slowly at first and then in a cascade is remarkable and very satisfying. The juice careers off into a large stainless steel open tub from whence it is pumped automatically into the latest vat.

The poetry is in the pressing, and the long hours of repetitive work can be like a gymnasium or callisthenics. The rhythm can be very satisfying and you can almost build a cheese in a trance, or if you wish hold a deep conversation with your opposite number. The conversations at times can be very interesting but you always have to keep your wits about you. There are many things to watch out for, apart from the machinery noise of four or five different machines. Any slight change in pitch may mean something very nasty.

It is hard work but much quicker than the old process of squeezing one cheese a day between straw, which is what farm workers used to do in the early evening, when they returned from the land, and then tweak it last thing at night and first thing in the morning, then unload it the next evening, before building the next cheese. Some cut round with a hay knife and make up a second layer, others press a second time and in the past made what was called 'water cider' which was like 'small beer', made from reacquainting the pomace with boiled water, then pressing out a second time. It was fit for children, and quick consumption at harvest time.

Some have old wooden presses with screw threads that are wound down with a series of gears or with a long spanners about seven feet long. Lorry jacks are very useful off three or four ton tippers. The pressure has to be even. These are the impressive beasts that you see in museums or lurking in sheds. Few are still in operation but in their day they were worshipped like good cart horses, and just as strong and good-looking. The sight of an old press in the half shadows is like a medieval siege machine or some infernal device from the Spanish Inquisition. They are masterpieces of agricultural engineering, simple, effective and stand the test of time. They needed good long straw without pesticides or growth retarders and a good supply of willing workers. But the presses we use give three or four times the pressure and there isn't the need to repress a second or even a third time. The cider press is like a magnet it draws people from far and wide and they watch transfixed for hours as the juice pours out, juice that tastes far better than anything you might have tasted before. It is pure nectar and comes out a kind of ruddy brown and in the sunlight glistens like honey. A cascade of juice, a river in flood. Pure magic...

One friend of mine in Dorset, called Simon, in the village of Burton Bradstock, actually lived in a hole in the ground with his cider press, a fine example of a double screw thread, which had come on a lorry from Cannington. It was so big he had to dig down about eight or nine feet and over the top of it he built a wattle, daub and thatch hut, like a Saxon short house, and in one end of this he lived with his lurcher called Rosie. There was room for the odd barrel, a cooking stove, a mattress for a bed, a small library and some sheep shearing equipment. This state of affairs went on for a winter or two, but the hole was near a stream and it did have a tendency to flood. The press is now in the middle of

Dorset near Fontmell Magna and the hut, well that burnt down due to an excess of fat in the sausages... or so I was told... The dog you will be glad to hear like its owner is still alive and well.

But the big hydraulic presses, when they've got up to pressure and finished the job, the engine is stopped, the valve released and the cheese let down. It is then trundled out to the far end of the cider house where it is off loaded layer by layer. In the old days when presses were not as strong or vigorous, they would make the *ciderkin*, and in the *Cyder Poem* of 1708, there is a good description of this process...

"Some, when the Press by utmost Vigour screwed
Has drained the pulpous Mass, regale their swine
With the dry refuse; thou more wise, shalt steep
Thy husks in Water, and again employ
The ponderous engine. Water will imbibe
The small remains of Spirit, and acquire
A vinous flavour; this the peasants blith
Will quaff, and whistle, as thy tinkling Team
They drive... Nor shalt thou now
Reject the Apple Cheese, tho' quite exhaust
Ev'n now twill cherish, and improve the Roots
Of sickly plants; new Vigour hence conveyed
Will yield an harvest of unusual Growth."

Indeed the quantities of pomace from a large cider farm are enormous and they should be re-cycled as soon as possible as great clamps of it turn black and gungey. One dairy farmer swears by it for his cows and it doesn't seem to taint the milk. So cheeses are built pressed and unloaded, hour after hour, day after day, week after week all over the South West.

From blossom to cider press to Daisy's gut. The relentless agricultural cycle, upon which our landscape thrives, and in the pomace lie the seeds, the pectin, the DNA.

St Guenole (414-504) of Brittany chose to chastise himself by living on a diet of water and perry, and other ascetics in the sixth and seventh centuries, braver still, chastised themselves by living on perry alone...

RK French : The History and Virtues of *Cyder* 1982

Cider and Perry are notable beverages in sea voyages...
A wonderful and refreshing drink... an assured remedy for sicknesse taken at sea.

Francis Bacon *New Atlantis* 1626

Part Four

Dark Secrets - The Vatican

This part of the cider farm is not, in Rome, but it does have a large number of wooden vats, hence its name. For the Pope substitute the Apple God and if you want to be true to Roman form, swap the Virgin Mary for Pomona the Apple Goddess, who apart from trying to keep herself intact, was pretty good with the pruning hook and all the arts associated with the culture of orchards. Indeed Ovid mentions her in his *Metamorphoses* as a wood nymph. Maybe after all Eve was an enlightened and liberated Pomona, and the apple originally associated not so much with guilt, as good honest healthy pleasure. The fruit of life in all senses of the word. Pomona's annual festival or feast just happens to coincide with the Celtic festival of Samhain and the Christian one of All Souls's Eve, the now somewhat reverted pagan Hallowe'en at the end of October, which is fairly close to the modern Apple Day, October 21st. So if Pomona the Goddess has the orchard, then the God has the Vatican, this is where he reigns supreme, this is his territory the inner sanctum, the dark workings within the cave. It is here that the cider is fermented and stored, it is here that the cider apples undergo their transformation, the resurrection.

"Their ransomed juice pumped to distant vats
Vast in their yeast brooding,
Potent and powerful, broad in the beam,
Fecund and fattening,
Their froth fermenting bellies,
Bound with oak and straps of iron
Barrels, giant and gargantuan."

It is the scale of the thing which impresses. One vat, called Huge Vat, holds nigh on 10,000 gallons and is as big as a small house. Ten thousand gallons which, at half a gallon a day, would have taken a farm labourer just over fifty four years years to drink, i.e. his whole working life or on a large farm of 27 labourers and one boy, it would have lasted at least two years. But then the ration increased to six or even eight pints a day at harvest time. Cider was valued at 6d a gallon so if a man was drinking 4 pints day for six days a week, that was 3 gallons a week which was equivalent to 1/6 extra on his pay packet of 9/- a week... a significant increase. Or, if you look at it another way an extra day's pay per week, or an extra 52 days pay per year, a not insubstantial sum.

If you look at it in today's rates, 3 gallons @ £4 a gallon is an extra £12 a week or £208 pound a year. But then a day's pay today is worth more than 3 gallons of cider. In fact a day's pay @ £4 an hour is £32, so in real terms measured against the cider barometer, farm pay has increased $2\frac{1}{2}$ times since Tolpuddle. In fact the trouble with Tolpuddle was that farm wages went down from 9/- to 8/- and then 7/6 a week. I doubt if the farmer's port consumption dipped at all.

Indeed cider, as mentioned earlier, was a double-edged sword. It was good in moderation, it helped a man and woman to get through what were appalling living conditions, the worst in Europe according to Cobbett and he was not given to exaggeration... but once a farm hand was hooked on cider, his overtime, particularly at harvest, was paid in cider, when he and his wife would probably have preferred the good honest chink of coin against coin in sweaty palm.

Cider was fine but it didn't feed starving children. There was a small potato famine in Somerset just before the Irish famine, and one landowner, with characteristic aplomb, upon smelling the rotting potatoes is reported to have said, that, "*there is nothing wrong with the potatoes that a little curry powder wouldn't cure*". It is a miracle that there wasn't a full scale rebellion, but that's another story.

In fact *Captain Swing* and the riots in the 1830's, which preceded the Tolpuddle affair, no doubt weighed heavily on the magistrates' minds when they sentenced the six men to hard labour in a distant colony. The farmers kept their labourers on the edge of malnutrition for several reasons. The main point being that they hadn't got the energy to rebel. The farmworkers had no vote and were preached at by clergymen who were living out of the gentry's pocket... which is why Methodists, Baptists, Quakers, Unitarian Churches and United Reformed, mostly chose Ministers from their own flock, and were very popular and influential, particularly in the West Country.

Trading cider for labour was known as *truck*, a term used for exchanges of other goods, which suited the owner rather than the employee. In the period of industrialisation and particularly in mining districts where tin, copper, lead, iron and other metals were of little use to a family, they came up with the idea of trade tokens which you then spent at the company's shop. A good system on the face of it, but it depended on who was setting the prices. They do however provide an intriguing and valuable look at industrial and rural England at this time.

The only option the labourers had was either the poor house, religion or emigration. *Blessed* are the meek for they shall inherit the earth. *Blessed* are the poor for they shall suffer in silence : the biggest con of all time. *Blessed* are the gentry for they shall inherit more than their fair share without lifting a finger... *Blessed* are the apple trees, for they shall bring forth blossom and cider.

Cider drinking, religion and the threat of the yeomanry kept the population submissive, and there was no doubt a fair difference in quality between what ended up on the master's table and what was sent out into the field every day... to sustain working men. Meat was infrequent as one report from a shepherd's wife makes clear in 1867, and this from a *"close"* or enclosed parish near Blandford. The shepherd's wife was obviously frightened to give her name or her sons' names or even the village's name, but her testimony is one of the most heart wrenching and honest in the report... about meat in her family she says this :

"We don't get a bit of butcher's meat, not for half a year, not from Christmas to Christmas; we sometimes get a bit of mutton at 3d the lb, when a giddy sheep is killed on the farm, it is good when sticked in time; sometimes we buy a bit at Christmas. We have a pig; sometimes we kill perhaps two in the year. We live on potatoes, bread and pig meat, and are very thankful if we can get a bit of pigmeat; we often sit down to dry bread. For harvest dinner we sent out for some boiled potatoes, a bit of cabbage and we put a bit of fat to the potatoes, I don't know if butcher's meat ever goes out to the harvest field. They drink cocoa at harvest. We never have a bit of milk. They used to have what they called chickory, and we drinked a good bit of it. But now it seems to have gone away. In the evening they sit down to what they have got, sometimes a bit of bread, cheese and butter. They are very fond of butter. They drink tea, we give 6d and 8d for a quarter of a pound of tea."

So no cider drunk here, or if it was, it wasn't mentioned, though money for beer was given @ 2d a day but 4d a day for June, July and August. There was a brewery in Blandford that is still going. It is always easy at a distance to criticise the drinking habits of an impoverished working class but very often with no hope of improvement there was little other way out. With such harsh working hours and conditions and capital punishments it is little wonder cider was held in such regard. Clergymen waged a campaign to reduce their dependence on cider but it was in some parts an uphill struggle and their right to cider actively defended.

But we digress from the Vatican... Instead of all taxes going to Rome they stay in this country now. Returns are made, paper work filled out, the Customs and Excise, Inland Revenue and VAT placated. In fact in the sixties and seventies many farmers gave up making cider because they couldn't cope with decimalisation and the paperwork. A few I am sure could not read or write... but knew every gallon and every tree and every sheep and every ditch on the farm.

But the barrels and the vats are the important things and they all have to be checked for leaks. A cooper is brought in as the season progresses to check them over, as many of the barrels have seen several seasons abroad. The best are 'two year' sherry barrels, and it is these that Scotch Whisky is matured in, to give, colour, oak and flavour. When cleaning out the big vats care has to be taken in case the oxygen levels get too low. Its a long way up the ladder again and there are stories of people falling asleep in vats after having a little too much to drink and getting plimmed up for good.

But the main job is getting the yeast to start and each vat is prepared 24 hours before hand with a brew that is already on the go. Once the cider apple juice is pumped to its particular vat, it starts working with the natural yeasts and a great brown head soon forms and a fair bit of heat as well. The cider 'works', which in fact is eating away at the sugar in the juice which is turned into alcohol... this is where chemistry becomes very useful.

To climb up a sixteen foot ladder and peer over the top a large vat is to look down upon a desert, there is nothing to give the eye any perspective and it looks just like Saudi Arabia from 30,000 ft, slightly undulating brown hills far below. The fermentation process uses up oxygen and gives off carbon dioxide... which if it is bottle fermented will yield small bubbles. Apparently nitrogen and high pressure makes the bubbles smaller, which is what you are looking for in a sparkling cider, sometimes this happens naturally in a normal barrel, although not to any great extent.

To start a batch off in the old days people would float yeast on a piece of dried toast, as they would place in a cider tree at wassailing time, to kick-start the brew, and to bring life symbolically back to the orchard. This process of fermentation must have seemed like a miracle which in a sense it is, the secret is to keep the fermentation pure and not to let it become too yeasty and to kill of the subtle flavours of the cider. Cloudy cider does not keep well and the invasion of 'frit' flies can send a whole batch to vinegar very easily. Cider vinegar is good and second to none but you don't need 10,000 gallons of it.

Old ways of keeping the fermentation pure were to put in shavings of fir, oak or beech, or a little bit of quick lime, powder of calcined flints, alabaster, white marble or rock allum. If that didn't cure it, then use isinglass said to be a corruption of *hausenblase* or sturgeon's bladder. More commonly isinglass is made from the gelatin of hooves. So even in Worlidge's day they were up to all sorts of tricks... as well as using glass syphons for racking off the cider without disturbing the sediment...

About syphoning off, this description from the *Cyder Poem* of 1708 describes the process marvellously :

"*Suffice it to provide a brazen Tube*
Inflext ; self taught, and voluntary flies
The defecated Liquor, thro' the Vent
Ascending, then by downward tract convey'd
Spouts into subject Vessels, lovely clear
As when a Noon-tide sun with Summer beams

Darts through a cloud, her watry Skirts are edg'd
With lucid Amber; or undrossy Gold
So, and so richly the purg'd Liquid shines."

Descriptions which are landscapes in themselves, and no doubt the best cider was used to impress the ladies of the house. Indeed certain barrels were sweetened with raisins and the like, for their own use. For the rough cider, however, hops, turnips, rice, parsnips and else to hand was used... When your cider is '*ropey*' or '*mothery*' you know you are well on the way to making cider vinegar, which although it does not attract tax, doesn't quite taste the same, though with honey it is supposed to cure arthritis and all manner of other complaints, far cheaper than the NHS.

As for vessels Worlidge advocates the larger the better, and there are several ways to purify the cask. Scalding water is one, or if it is musty, add pepper, or you can use quicklime mixed in a few gallons and swirled around, or as Worlidge puts it delicately :

"To make your cask pleasant, to receive so delicate a guest as your choicest cider, you may scent it as the vintners do their wines. Thus take Brimstone four ounces of burned alum one ounce and Aquae vitae two ounces, unrectified or ardent spirits of the first distillation. Melt these together in an earthen pan over hot coals then dip therein a piece of new canvas and instantly sprinkle thereon the powders of nutmeg, cloves, coriander and aniseed. This canvas set on fire and let it burn in the bung hole so as the fume may be received in the vessel."

A marvellous recipe which would fumigate any uncertainty in the barrel, spiritual or otherwise.

The forces at work are at times subtle and at others enormous. The power and force of the cider must not be underestimated. The vat which holds 10,000 gallons contains 100,000 lbs, for a gallon weighs 10 lbs, which means that there is 44 tons of cider and then there is the head, the vapours which will burst any sealed vessel. The secret is to let the fermentation bubble away quietly on its own without letting in any new air, an upturned bottle, spout down helps and fits well into any bung hole... The expression '*tunning up*' does not mean going flat out on your motorbike, but filling up a vessel to near its top but allowing enough room for the head to work. A tun is the same as two pipes or four hogsheads. Even when a bung is placed in, a small hole must be left... Worlidge advocates putting in a quart of unground wheat to a hogshead which gives it an artificial head, wheat that it might have got naturally from the straw for making the cheeses.

The mention of vessels, tunning up, preparing barrels and preserving cider, was of course vital for those seeking sustenance on long voyages. And in the dark depths of the Vatican, it is not unlike being in the hold of a small cargo ship at anchor. The swell is well within one's capabilities, but with oceans of cider to port and starboard, drowning is still a faint possibility...

The importance of cider and apples on long sea voyages has perhaps been overlooked in the past and deserves more attention. That large quantities of cider or *Sider* were taken, is clear from the account already mentioned in 1620, being Richard Whitbourne's 'Discourse' on his Discovery and settlement of '*a plantacion to the benefitt of fishing of NEW-FOUND-LAND...*' The Charge i.e. the list of stores and food taken for 32 persons includes *Twenty Six Tunne of Beere and Sider @ 53 shillings 4 pence the tunne, which comes to 69 li 6s 8d i.e.* about 16% of the fitting out bill. Richard Whitbourne who was from Exmouth and no doubt knew the qualities of his *Sider* that would keep well... indeed the cider made from Devon apples in the old way and well stored had high Vitamin C content but land and sea scurvy were not the only problem, for Richard Whitbourne also refers to the problems of *French Pyrates* and *Sea Rousers* and *erring Subjects* who were likely to relieve one of the entire catch of salt cod almost within sight of home, as happened off Lisbon in 1616 to the value of 860 pounds, the guilty party being one Daniel Tibolo. No doubt Drake who was born near Tavistock also knew a thing or two about cider... and piracy... and the pleasurable aspects of both.

Significantly perhaps the one part of Newfoundland that they colonised was called the *Avalon* peninsular and there was even a ship called the *Ark of Avalon* at Dartmouth in 1627... Maybe also it is no chance that the apple moved from cod fisheries off Newfoundland into the St Lawrence river and thus started the orchards there, an industry that survives to this day. Even Breton and Dorset folk tunes have gone backwards and forwards, as well as the art of distilling... One well known Devon company, *Whiteways* of Whimple, who had supplied Edward VII, Sir Arthur Conan Doyle and WG Grace, also had a stake in The *Annapolis Cyder Company Ltd*. Bridgetown, Nova Scotia in the twenties. An interesting link which gave them insight into 'American' marketing methods and commercial approach which later stood them in good stead.

Another reference, in the eighteenth century, but also from Devon, gives insight, into the value of good cider, particularly when warmer climes are envisaged... this reference from 1720...

" *The merchants, who go great voyages to sea, find it a very useful drink in their ships and so buy up great store of it; for one ton of cider will go as far as three of beer and is found more wholesome in hot climates*"

T Cox

Reports from Anson's voyage around the world in the 1740's and salutary tales about the ravages of scurvy were not lost on sailors back home. In April 1741 he lost 43 men to scurvy and in May twice that number... No doubt the cider had run out round Cape Horn, if indeed he took any at all... just cause for mutiny, which did in fact occur. But then Anson had set out from Portsmouth. If he had gone from Plymouth, no problem, though there is a very good Hampshire apple called the *Hambledon Deux Ans*, which keeps for two years and would have lasted him half his voyage...

It may well be that only the merchants and cyderists could see the logic and not the Board of Admiralty... Rum and the Surgeon's '*pellets*' would have do... The navy were very slow learners as lemon juice was actually first used successfully in 1605 on an East Indiaman named appropriately *The Dragon*. A quarter of the other ship's crews who did not take lemon juice were lost, whereas *The Dragon* lost not a single man.

A few years later in the 1620's none other than Francis Bacon was drawing attention to the fact that :

"Cider and Perry are notable beverages for sea voyage..."
"...an assured remedy for sicknesse taken at sea"

and an advised greeting with oranges for those upon first stepping ashore after a long voyage.

Another interesting maritime account comes from a despatch dated 25 Sept 1759 the year of victories, which shows that sailors from Hawke's squadron when they were re-supplied with a shipload of apples, law and order broke down completely and the apples were :

"immediately plundered by the men before the pursers could take any account of it..."

An interesting scene no doubt... but it shows the power of apples over naval discipline, and no doubt it also shows the power of the association of home that the sailors must have had whilst on blockade, as well as the incipient fear of scurvy and the desire for fresh fruit. That apples were better favoured than the other alternative of *sauerkraut*, as a preventative, is I think without doubt, though the German Navy might have disputed this if it had been in existence then.

Capt. Cook who was the son of an agricultural worker and later worked with a shopkeeper in Whitby, in Yorkshire before setting out on his career afloat, fully realised the importance of the apple. Curiously enough some old varieties have turned up around Whitby some of which can be kept for two years, highly useful... the *Ribston Pippin* is also very high in Vitamin C. These apples would have been kept in barrels.

Other interesting items from Yorkshire to do with the sea and apples have been recorded by George Morris of Stonegrave. Firstly, that there was a certain apple called the *Hunt House* in 1831 which thrived on the North York Moors and was used to supply the Whitby fishing fleets. Whalers had also by necessity to be away for long periods. And secondly, there is tell of one intrepid trader, called '*Kipper*' of Kirkby Moorside who would walk with apples to Whitby, exchange them for kippers and then trudge home again with the kippers on his back, a distance of at least twenty miles over rough moorland. It must have kept him fit and healthy and never short of a good meal...

But to return to Captain Cook, it was only five months after the burial of his body at sea off Hawaii in 1779, that the Royal Navy eventually orders fruit juices to be used aboard its ships, an order that had to wait till 1795 to become compulsory. It is fact only in this century that the true nature of Vitamin C and its deficiency has been truly understood. And indeed not all cider is rich in it, and oxidisation can deplete the Vitamin C content surprisingly quickly. But to first get your limes you had to have access to large plantations in the West Indies, and that required settlement.

Ironically the Mediteranean was stuffed full of lemons and lemon juice was twice as good as lime juice, but limes were smaller and tougher...

Apples had in a sense filled the gap, but could not keep whole fleets free of scurvy in the tropics for long periods of time, and anyway lime juice was far more concentrated and took up less room below decks. But the cider apple had no doubt played its part in the development of trade overseas and what later became to be called *The Empire*... and with trade and emigration went the apple, or to be more precise the cuttings, the hard graft.

All apples were in all senses of the word home-grown. Indeed the apple later went as far afield as New Zealand as well, but as the nineteenth century agriculturists and farm workers were predominantly law abiding, tee totalling, non-conformists, they missed a golden opportunity and tended to plant only dessert apples, rather than the cider apple. The gap was slowly filled by their now, very successful wine industry... No doubt the whaling fleets and the whole of the South Pacific would have benefited, but their trips ashore though colourful were infrequent, and you would have had to have had a fair quantity on tap...

The apple in one sense was lucky that it could migrate at the zenith of the industry in this country, and so great care was taken in choosing varieties, and sites for orchards. No doubt great histories about apple emigration have yet to be written...

But to return from the voyage at 'sea' so to speak, and the digression on scurvy and the hold it must have had on people's imaginations, we must once more enter the quiet, dark recesses of the Vatican, where we once again meet John Worlidge who is, as always, trying to perfect the process of purity and preservation. In 1678 he is not averse to using sulphur for scenting the cask, which he does :

"by letting the canvas in with brimstone by way of a wire into the vessel, fume it vigorously and then tunnup immediately, It gives it no ill taste or flavour, and is an excellent preserver of your health as well as your liquor."

Even today nearly all cider makers, wine makers and home made beer fanatics, used sodium meta bi-sulphite to purify their casks and equipment, so nothing much has changed... It was said that the monks of Tavistock Abbey were in league with the Devil because he had taught them how to make good sweet cider by using brimstone... no doubt to purify their equipment and stop the wilder yeasts taking over completely.

In the Vatican, each cask, each vat is made of oak, the large ones are from eight to sixteen feet high and the same in diameter. The vertical oak slats are bound with wire hawsers that can be tensioned if necessary. Some of the vats are French and these are wonderful oval barrels on end. They exude charm and provide good cider. Others more modern are made from stainless steel or fibre glass, less exotic but fine so long as the cider is allowed to spend a decent amount of time in the oak before being sold. Oak definitely adds character to the cider was well as some colour.

This period of fermentation is crucial for if a vat goes off in a different direction vast amounts are wasted. This is where the balance of *bitter sweets* and *bitter sharps* is necessary. Six to eight weeks is the usual time for fermentation but this depends on the sugar levels and the outside temperature. If all goes well the sound of odd bubbling noise in the dark is music to a cidermaker's ears. The sheer volume of cider, the wealth displayed, the harvest stored. That is satisfaction enough, even before the testing... the blending and distilling.

The Vatican is a place of pure magic, nature bountiful, the hand of the Apple God and Goddess Pomona their virtues shared, the toast offered. The Vatican is the deposit account, the grainstore, the tithe barn, the security, a message that all is well on the farm... hints of future revelling, maidens undone in the orchards come full circle, baptised with the heathen apple... Adam's apple and Eve's bust... Cider does the rounds, and a good farmer looks after his vats, like a devoted priest, always checking for leaks and checking that each of the vats is well on its way. This is where the fine tuning of cidermaking is done. This is, as it were, the other end of the orchard, the end result. The golden tap that you hope never runs dry...

Then put a pound and a half of pure double refined sugar in powder, which will soon dissolve in that hot liquor... then put it into bottles ; and after a little time it will be a most pleasant, quick, cooling smoothing drink. Excellent in sharp *Gonorrhoeas*.

Sir Kenelm Digby   1603-1665

If you add a small quantity of Loaf-sugar more or less according as it may require, it will give new life to the Cider, and probably make it better than ever it was before...

When your cider is thus bottled... it is good to let the bottles stand a while before you stop them close. Observe that when a bottle breaks through the fermentation of the Cider, to open your corks and give vent... Great care is to be taken in choosing good corks...

John Worlidge 1678

Part Five

TO SPARKLE OR NOT TO SPARKLE...

This is perhaps one of the more interesting debates in the cider world and it has implications far beyond the cider house...

The word *cider* itself covers a variety of drinks. There is of course the dry, medium and sweet farmhouse ciders, usually flat but with a hint of autumn gold. These are, or should be, naturally fermented on the farm from cider apples and matured in oak. Some of these can be exceptional and are the true ciders... The strongest ciders are often the driest, because all the sugar has turned to alcohol, and one man's *medium* maybe another man's *dry*. Good dry cider is an acquired taste but the dryness should not be confused with sharpness, which is associated with acetic acid, or vinegar. The skill of the old cider makers, which was very considerable, was to get a fermentation that still retained some of the natural sweetness, and at the same time to kept the more undesirable reactions at bay... The secret is still to keep the balance of sharpness there in the beginning, hence the ratio between *bitter sharps* and *bitter sweets* in any given batch or even orchard, and each apple however uninspring it may look has its use... and the cider apple season is long. At each point the balance has to be made. Some apples like *Morgan Sweet*, an early apple, can be used in single variety ciders which are the *Beaujolais* of the cider world, and are ready for drinking in late November or early December, which is useful to fill the 'hungry gap'. Often we are drinking it whilst still making the tail end of the main batch... and very welcome it is too. But these early ciders generally do not keep or travel well, but can at times be exceptional and very welcome as the first 'bite'. Occasionally they do sparkle when young, which can be very refreshing but the sparkle does not last forever...

Other single variety ciders like *Kingston Black* and *Stoke Red* can be made in the old style bottle fermented method which produces a sparkling cider and is quite rightly alluded to as the '*Champagne*' of the south west, though that word has its own problems. John Worlidge with his usual attention to detail devotes six pages to this method and talks about how best to store the bottles and advocates the interesting concept of having a conservatory with '*access to cysterns of running spring water to cool the bottles*' and they will over time he says '*mature as strong as canary wine.*'

Indeed the history of bottle fermented cider is fascinating and there is ample proof given by Tom Stevenson in his recent book on Champagne, that the so called '*Methode Champenoise*' was invented here in England. Certainly it was being made on a large scale by 1662 when the famous eight page paper by Christopher Merret was deposited at the Royal Society, a paper that mentions the fact that :

"Our wine coopers of later times use vast quantities of sugar and molasses to all sorts of wines, to make them drink brisk and sparkling & to give them the spirit..."

and this as Tom Stevenson points out, predates any real

French claim by several years if not decades... The wording is also interesting because of the use of the term '*later times*', and also the word '*vast*' which appeals to me... implying that a large scale industry is under way and that the addition of sugar was a deliberate act to induce a secondary fermentation. The quote goes on further to add that this technique also '*mends their bad facts*' which in a sense implies that it may well have been found accidentally in experiments to remedy bad wine. The word '*sugar*' is mentioned many times. The paper also makes the comment that '*Country vintners feed their fretting wines with raw beef...*' which to me would imply that the process was done within a barrel as you would with cider...

There is in fact no actual mention of bottling in the paper, but wine was commonly bottled in England from Shakespeare's day onwards. They had the cork and wine would travel. But it was the invention of the much stronger bottle glass which is of interest, and this as an indirect result of conservation measures taken by James I and a somewhat corrupt Admiral, called Sir Robert Mansell, who was Treasurer to the Navy 1604-18. Patronage was rife and he made a fair packet giving favours and appointments in return for back handers. Timber in particular was sold to the Navy at double the going rates through his hands... As timber began to run out, Sir Robert persuaded his King, friend and Protector, James I, to make a law in 1615, prohibiting the use of charcoal for glass making and then iron smelting. Timber for barrel making was however still allowed, and much of this came from Ireland.

This decision to stop the use of charcoal was not as altruistic as it may at first seem, as its real function was not to so much to protect the forests of the realm for the Navy, but so that Sir Robert and James I could still make a bit on the side... Plundering woodlands was a favourite upper class occupation to pay off debts and extravagant lifestyles.

In fact, the Parliament later brought in an early version of the Forestry Commission. The curious side effect of not being allowed to use charcoal resulted in the use of coal in the glass making process which gave a higher temperatures and meant that the glass makers could get a thicker glass. Venetian glass although made in London since the 1570's, was decorative but not strong. Durability and the ability to withstand the rigours of transport on rough roads and afloat were more important, particularly where bottles were concerned.

In 1620 Sir Robert Mansell, having plundered his own nation, and lined his pocket, took to the ocean wave at last and finished off his Naval career by an unsurpassed display of incompetence, where he allowed a bunch of Algerian pirates to run rings round him. Sensing opposition, he then at last retired from the Navy and set up his own glass works protected by Royal patent, and so the story goes, whilst experimenting with coloured glass, added a combination of iron and manganese which made it much tougher. Whether he did it himself, or just happened to own the glassworks is not clear, but he had, in effect, invented the pre-cursor to bottle glass, which was not only coloured but reinforced.

Another man also credited with experimentation with bottle glass at the same time is Sir Kenelm Digby, 1603-1665, Gentleman, writer and wit, and this in the 1630's, in Gloucestershire, possibly at Newland-on-Wye ideally situated above the Wye valley. Five essential ingredients were there. A history of wine and cider making, a tradition of glass making to draw on from Bristol and Gloucester and even Bridgwater. Ancient coalfields in the Forest of Dean which was used in preference to charcoal, a sharp intellect, and a river navigation with the sea at one end, and at the other, Hereford and Mr Scudamore. Otherwise known as Lord Scudamore of Holme Lacy in Herefordshire who had already imported the famous

Redstreak after his sojourn in France, where he had stayed two years as Charles Ist's Ambassador...

This bottle glass then provided the admirable vehicle for experimentation with secondary fermentation, a process which I am sure was commonly used in cider circles, to enliven cider and improve it. or in the words of John Worlidge :

" *If Cider be acid, as sometimes happens, by reason of immaturity of the fruit, too nimble an operation, too great a fermentation in the vessel, or too warm a situation of your vessels, wherein it is kept; this sometimes becomes plesasant again... But the surest remedy is Bottling it with a Knob of Sugar in proportion according to the occasion...*"

And this in 1676. Indeed the very term *wine* is used somewhat loosely at this time and the very title of John Worlidge's book *Vinetum Brittanicum or a Treatise on Cider* implies that there must have been considerable interplay and even rivalry between the two areas of interest.

These details of bottle fermenting cider would not have been worked out overnight and it is not beyond the bounds of possibility that the experiments were conducted in the country estates of Gloucestershire and Herefordshire by those Royalists who after the Civil War, if they did not go to the continent, must have retired to their walled gardens and kept their heads down during the Commonwealth and Protectorate. And when these 'Puritan' times ended and the delights of the Restoration were in full swing, they re-emerged and gave free range to their scientific experiments, and trials in husbandry. Writing papers, books and extolling the virtues of their new found confidence in the fruits of the nation.

One such treasure trove of investigations is that belonging Sir Kenelm Digby himself (1603 - 1665) whose Closet, or close papers, were only published four years after his death in 1669, under the engaging title of *Sir Kenelm Digby's Closet Opened*. by H Broome at the *Star* in Little England. Sir Kenelm had a colourful life, his father Sir Everard, was implicated in the gunpowder plot and was hung, drawn and quartered. Sir Kenelm's life is mentioned at length in *Brief Lives* by none other than John Aubrey... Kenelm Digby was educated at Gloucester Hall Oxford, later joined the Navy, courted Venetia Stanley, as half of Europe seems to have done, married her secretly, got Knighted, became a pirate, wins a famous victory at Scanderoon, became Surveyor General of the Navy, wrote his memoirs, poisoned his wife accidentally with a broth of vipers, had her painted in bed by Van Dyck, while she lay there inert, so to speak, and then spent the rest of his life being banished, either to his closet, which was in fact his laboratory and study, or had to flee abroad, and all the time collected a multitude of recipes and alcoholic concoctions... He spoke at least 10 languages, and in the last years of his life became a Council member of the Royal Society. He is also credited with preserving English Medieval Literature by depositing copius manuscripts in the Bodelian at Oxford.

What is of real interest to the investigator of bottle fermented cider and wine, is the 90 or so pages he devotes to the alcoholic beverages, and their recipes which include among other things :

TO MAKE ALE DRINK QUICK

When small Ale hath wrought sufficiently, draw into bottles; but first put into every bottle twelve good raisins of the Sun split and stoned... Then stop up the bottle close, set it in sand (gravel) or a cold dry Cellar. After a while this will drink exceeding quick and pleasant. Likewise take six Wheat-corns, and bruise them and put them into a bottle of Ale; it will make it exceeding quick and stronger.

i.e. a secondary bottle fermented process. What is interesting about his notes is that they are in fine detail, and it has been asserted that the original work was published, with his son John's consent, by his steward and laboratory assistant George Hartman. This in 1669, and again in 1671 and 1677. His second son, a fine swordsman, died fighting in 1644, for the King's cause at Bridgwater...

This description of perking up Ale is then closely followed by a description of how to make cider...

TO MAKE CIDER

Take a Peck of Apples, and slice them, and boil them in a barrel of water, till the third part be wasted. Then cool your water as you do for wort, and when is cold you must pour the water upon three measures of grown Apples. Then draw forth the water at a tap three or four times a day, for three days together. Then press out the Liquor and Tun it up; when it hath done working, then stop it up close.

Then he makes what he calls :

A VERY PLEASANT DRINK OF APPLES

Take about fifty pippins; quarter and core them, without paring them... treat them in a similar way as above, more or less, and then... and he sounds like Mrs Beaton here...

Put to them a pound and a half of pure double refined Sugar in powder, which will soon dissolve in that hot liquor. Then pour it into a Hippocras bag, and let it run through it two or three times, to be very clear. Then put it into bottles; and after a little time, it will be a most pleasant, quick, cooling smoothing drink. Excellent in sharp **Gonorrhoeas**.

I doubt if the modern *White Ciders* would cure *Gonorrhoea* so easily, but if they did it would cheaper than all that anti-biotic which we today consume either knowingly or unknowingly...

Then follows another interesting description of cidermaking in which bottling is described in some detail... This is possibly, the Neale of *Neale's yard* in London. Maybe he did his experiments there...

SIR PAUL NEALE'S WAY OF MAKING CIDER

The best Apples make the best Cider, as Pearmains, Pippins, Golden Pippins, and the like. Codlings make the finest Cider of all. They must be ripe, when you make cider of them; and is in prime in the summer season, when no other Cider is good. But lasteth not long beyond Autumn. The foundation of making perfect **CYDER** *consisteth in not having it work much, scarce ever at all; but at least, no second time; which Ordinary Cider doth often, upon change of weather, and upon motion; and upon every working it grows harder. Do then thus :*

There then follows is a description of what is known in Devon and West Somerset as *Kieving* which is starting the fermentation but then straining the partially fermented liquid off before it takes bad ways and trying very hard not to let the air get to it. A process also of clarification and ridding the liquid of its grosser sediment. Then after a day or two follows the bottling :

When it is clear enough draw it into bottles, filling them within two fingers, which stop close. After two or three days visit them; that if there be a danger of their working (which would break the bottles) you may take out the stopples, and let them stand open for half a quarter of an hour. Then stop them close, and they are secure for ever after. In cold freesing weather, set them upon Hay, and cover them over with hay or Straw. In open weather in Winter transpose them to another part of the Cellar to stand upon bare ground or pavement. In hot weather set them in sand. The Cider of the Apples of the last season, as Pippins, not Pearmains, nor codlings, will last till the summer grow hot. Though this never work, 'tis not of the Nature of **Strummed Wine**; *because* **the naughty dregs** *are not left in it.*

This description is detailed enough to show that experimentation had been carried out for a good number of years and what must be borne in mind is that these notes were published *after* Sir Kenelm's Digby's death, which occured in 1665. They may well have been written ten, twenty or even thirty years previously... which would make it much earlier than the French *'Champagne Method'*. One thing that interests me is the note at the end about *Strummed Wine* and *naughty dregs*, which one assumes are not the dregs of society, though they too could lead to ferment and revolt, the allusion is a powerful one, *naughty*, I suppose, because they can induce great pressure and the bursting of bottles and the shattering of not just one bottle but a whole cellar load. Hence they are desposited in sand, for if they explode they are as dangerous and lethal as *'jumping jacks'* and other venomous anti-personnel mines devised by the Americans during the Vietnam war... The term *Strummed Wine* derives, I think, from the Latin *Strum* or *Strumae* which means a swelling or cellular dilation... which could mean a number of things but most likely wine bottled up and permaturely exploding as Champagne would... It may be a term that was used for wine that became *Champagne* accidentally or was it induced deliberately ? It would be interesting to know whether *Strummed Wine* was a term of approval or disapproval...

In fact the removal of the *naughty dregs* these days has only been achieved through slowly turning the bottles so that the dregs are in the neck of the bottle which is then frozen with liquid nitrogen, and the pressure of the wine or cider behind, will push the plug out of its own accord. Re-bottling, topping up and the addition of a little sugar or honey can make it sparkle, fizz and erupt when the cork is at last removed at some Motor rally, tennis match, wedding or twenty first... In the old days the silvery, lead/tin foil which is part and parcel of Champagne look is in fact so designed to mask the top inch or two which is missing from the 'plug' having come out. When you shake it and open it you would never notice... *Champagne* bottles would make excellent heavy duty anti-tank *molotov* cocktails and shaped charges for demolitions...

But to return to Sir Kenelm Digby or to be more precise Doctor Harvey who has his own method of making :

DOCTOR HARVEY'S PLEASANT WATER CIDER

As above: *Take A Bushel of Pippins etc etc etc and strain through a Hypocras bag made of cotton*, which is a bag in the form of a salver suspended, ie to make it easier to pour through and then :

with the liquid almost cold sweeten it with five pound of Brown-sugar and put a pint of Ale-yest to it and set it working two days and nights: Then skim off the yest clean and put it into bottles, and let it stand two or three days, till the yest fall dead at the top: Then take it off clean with a knife, then fill it up a little within the neck, and then stop them up and tye them, or else it will drive out the Corks. Within a fortnight you may drink it. It will keep five or six weeks.

Many of the other recipes are for *Meade* and *Metheglin* which is a type of Welsh Meade made with honey...

There are rumours of a real cold snap in the 1630's and

this may, with late frosts, have decimated any vineyards that were left in this country at the time, and with France being the way it was, ie a long way off... the very best minds of the gentry were forced to experiment as they never had done before... to replace the gap left in their cellars not just by a Civil War, which no doubt sharpened their minds, but by the collapse of their own wine industry and society as they knew it, into the bargain. So naturally enough they turned their attentions from wine to the more resilient apple...

Suffice it to say that a little more investigation into archives might yield interesting fruit, and maybe ferment a bit of revolt across the channel. Those *naughty little dregs* which no doubt sparked the French Revolution 100 years later, may well have come from England after all. Thomas Paine ? the knock on effects in America and Ireland are being felt even today... we still talk about social ferment, situations bubbling over... One final concoction of Sir Kenelm's, also in the same mode, **CURRANTS WINE**, advocates the first fermentation :

with the purest and newest Ale-yest, Stop it very close till it ferment, then give such vent as is necessary, and keep it warm for about three days... taste it, to see if it be grown to your liking... As soon as you find it so, let it run through a strainer, to leave behind all the exhausted currants and the yeast, and so bottle it up. It will be exceeding quick and pleasant, and is admirable good to cool the Liver and cleanse the blood.

Interestingly one of the earliest recipes that he collected was called "*Sir Walter Raleigh's Great Cordial*". Sir Walter was executed in 1616 when Sir Kenelm was just 13. Interestingly the Digby's took over Sherborne Castle from Sir Walter and are still there today, though the Old Castle is no longer lived in, the New one is, with a marvellous lake and grounds.

But what of Sir Kenelm Digby ... ? He, alas, died of fever in Covent Garden, having been to France seeking a cure for gout and kidney stones. His *Closet* however is well worth investigating even though vipers may lurk there. The Van Dyck of his wife Venetia more dead than alive, is by the way in the National Portrait Gallery.

Certainly he was at the forefront of experimentation. Exile, a good war and the death of a spouse may well have encouraged him to pursue experiments in cookery which borderlined on alchemy... If anyone was said to have invented The '*Champagne' Method* in England, he would I think be a front runner, certainly his experiments in bottled beer, cider and wine show that he had a clear understanding of secondary fermentation and its associated problems. And anyway who knows how long his notes were lying around in his closet ? Sir Kenelm was a man of extraordinary qualities and I suspect of inventive mind.

What is also interesting and perhaps not generally known is that there was a also good tradition of wine making in Gloucestershire 100 years earlier in the sixteenth century as this excerpt from Camden's *Brittania* shows from 1586...

Here you may behold the highways and publick roads, full of fruit trees, not set, but growing naturally, The earth of its own accord bearing fruit, exceeding others both in taste and beauty, many of which continue fresh the whole year round, and serve the owner till he is supplied by new Increase. There is no province in England that hath so many, or so good Vineyards as this county, either for fertility or sweetness of the grape. The wine wereof carrieth no unpleasant tartness, being not much inferior to the French in sweetness...

Camden makes no mention of Cider but Edmund Gibson, his translator, from Latin into English, mentions in 1695 that the people of Herefordshire have :

an opportunity of making such vast quantities of Cyder, as not only to serve their own families, (for 'tis their general drink) but also to furnish London and other parts of England...

But before we leave that part of England, I cannot resist Camden's description of the River Severn, which I include, not only because it is wonderful, and the flooding reminiscent of Somerset, but because it gives some idea of the difficulty in transporting cider up and down the Severn with the Bore described as a *live beaste*, which is in ferment itself.

The river Severne... there is in it a daily rage and boisterousness of waters, which I know not wether I may call Gulph or Whirlpool, casting up the sands from the bottom and rowling them into heaps; it floweth with great torrent... but loses it force at the first bridge. Sometimes it overfloweth its banks, and wanders a great way into the neighbouring Plains and then returneth back as conqueror of the Land.

But to return to cider, the '*Methode Anglais*' as it should be called, and was called thus in France for many years, was a sophisticated process by 1676 with special racks, the bottles downward facing, or at least sideways to keep the corks moist, the positioning of cellars, the selection of corks, and of course the addition of sugar for the secondary fermentation... the variations of air and temperature, noted, mastered.

The meaner Cider is more apt to break your bottles than the richer... Observe that when a bottle breaks through the fermentation of the Cider to open your corks, and give vent, and stop them up again a while after, lest you loose many for want of caution... Great care is to be had in choosing good corks, much good liquor being absolutely spoiled through the

only defect of corks, therefore are glass stoppers to be preffered... if corks are steeped in boiling water a while, before you use them they will comply better with the mouth of the bottle than if forc'd in dry, also the moisture in the Cork doth advantage it in detaining the Spirits.

There is much else besides and wine experts could do worse than look in other cider letters, archives and manuscripts. Curiously the first literary reference to '*sparkling Champaign*' also occurs in 1676, in *The Man of Mode* by Sir George Etherege, a reference also mentioned by Tom Stevenson.

At no point in these earlier writings is there any reference to an equivalent French industry. An interesting point in 1678... Something for Europe to chew on.

Worlidge also mentions the process in relation to Currant wine... which is fermented with the aid of sugar, boiled, mixed with white wine, fermented, steadied, siphoned off and then within three weeks becomes :

so pure and limpid, that you may bottle it with a piece of Loaf sugar, in each bottles in bigness according to your discretion; which will not only abate its quick acidity, that it may as yet retain, but make it brisk and lively.

A passage that stands for itself. The word '*Champaign*' is not I think adopted in France till 1709, though '*Champaigne*' is mentioned in 1708 by John Phillips in his well known *Cyder Poem*, when referring to a farmer who regales his foreign guests with what they think is the best of continental :

*Some cyders have by Art, or Age unlearn'd
Their genuine relish, and of sundry Vines
Assumed the flavour; one sort counterfeits
The Spanish Product; this, to Gauls has seem'd.*

*The sparkling nectar of **Champaigne**: with that,*
A German oft has swill'd his Throat, and sworn,
Deluded that Imperial Rhine bestow'd
the Generous Rummer, whilst the Owner pleas'd
Laughs inly at his Guests, thus entertained
With Foreign Vintage from his Cyder Cask.

The first mention of the *Champagne* in the Shorter Oxford English Dictionary is 1664 with a quote from 1688, so Worlidge was pretty close, in 1676-8, The debate is an interesting one... and not without its controversy... particularly as Elderflower Champagne has come in for some stick recently.

A few bottle fermented ciders have come under the EEC axe recently being not yet officially exempt a devlish increase in duty from our own dear government, who have raised the tax 400%... The sparkling bottle fermented ciders are far more interesting than middle range champagne and half or a third the price... they are lovingly handled and turned eighteen times and like the Redstreak are made from single varieties... Kingston Black and Stoke Red, dry but with a wonderful rounded finish... with more than *'a hint of orchard on the tongue.'* A little sweeter perhaps and then they would be perfect.

Sacrilege though it may be to mention them in the same breath but these sparkling bottle fermented ciders are not in any way to be confused with other carbonated ciders or the so called new designer or *'yuppy'* ciders referred to earlier. These other concoctions are just below 8.5% in toxicity and have never apparently seen a cider apple. Rumour has it that at certain factories, a single cider apple is kept on a red cushion inside a safe in the Managing Director's office and every now and again brought out into the open and, on the same red cushion, is paraded round the works so that the essence of apple can permeate the brew...

It is interesting that on the so called designer ciders the word apple doesn't even appear and if it does it is printed so small you wouldn't even notice it. These high octane brews are fizzy bland and taste of *Golden Delicious*, which means they don't taste of anything... I have heard that *Golden Delicious* tastes very good in America but not in Europe. It just stores well and can withstand supermarket shelves, but that's all... No doubt the *'yuppy'* ciders are trying to emulate *Babycham* made from pears, which in its day, was an extraordinary success story. But that was in post-war England when champagne was relatively unobtainable. *Bambi* in Shepton Mallet... but *Showerings* have now sold out to *Gaymers*, who were in turn taken over by *Matthew Clark*, and they in turn have bought out *Taunton Cider* and have themselves been bought out by a US/Canadian drinks Giant. Just to confuse matters even more, *Taunton Cider* has itself, in the past, been owned by a whole string of Breweries, *Courages, Bass Charrington, Guinness, Scottish and Newcastle* and *Greene King*... so the cider world is as complex as the cider apple itself... .the market has changed... and is still changing. Conglomerates swallow each other, like pike, and usually orchards and farmers suffer. Even *Inch's* has gone metric, but occasionally Phoenix's do rise from the ashes... .

Then there are the so called *fizzy* ciders which are carbonated. These are much advertised and sold from what was *Taunton Cider*, Shepton Mallet and Hereford. *Dry Blackthorn, Strongbow and Woodpecker* spring to mind, pleasant enough if you are dying of thirst, after shearing 200 sheep, but probably only one third cider apples, the rest is apple concentrate from abroad, Eastern Europe and even China. The other concoctions which are called *white ciders* are, I am afraid, not much better than alcoholic lemonade. The big concerns may not like the *yokel* image but it is the *yokels* who had grafted in the orchards quite literally and kept the tradition alive... it is the *yokels* who have picked up the apples in all weathers and have worked the presses and made the cheeses in dark damp barns. Their work over hundreds of years, should not be dismissed lightly. In fact without the *yokels* there would be no cider industry at all, because it is they and their thirst, which have kept the orchards going through good times and bad, grafting, nurturing and experimenting.

At the other end of the cider scale many farmhouse ciders have devolved in the cloudy and vinegary ciders otherwise known as *scrumpy,* these are the ones that give cider a bad name and tourists a head ache. These are the ciders known as *'RAT''S PISS', 'GREEN BOGEY' 'HEN DROPPINGS' 'OLD CODJER'. 'DEAD DOG'* and *'GLOOMY FERRET'.* Eight pints a day will severely effect your judgement. In one cider house in Bristol clients paid for their first four pints and then got the next four on the house. These ciders have I suspect given the cider image a bad name and are a far cry from the fine ciders drunk in slender stemmed glasses decorated with apples and inlay work.

If you go across the Atlantic and mention *cider* in New York, the *Big Bad Apple,* you will only get apple juice. Real cider is called *hard cider.* Prohibition saw to that little trick, but even today you can always refer to this year's apple juice and last year's apple juice. and the *cognoscenti* will understand the difference.

In Normandy and Brittany of course you get good sparkling cider, and the process is strictly controlled. It may be that the path ahead is for cidermakers to set their own controls and abide by them and to exclude the more industrial methods of carbonisation, which was after all only brought in the thirties... and in a sense this gradually killed off the bottle fermented ciders.

It may well be that cider is even now undergoing the full transformation that real ale has, and will resurrect itself in the face of vast breweries and monopoly pub chains and cheap lager from across the channel. History is marvellous stuff, but like the cider it easily becomes cloudy. Now is the time to replant and the time to reassess the humble apple, to find out the old varieties. We lose our orchards and the skill of making first class cider at our peril.

Sadly the old cider farms, like the lights of Europe are going out one by one. It may take another generation of skilled and dedicated growers and producers to re kindle the flame, but hopefully it can be done before all the old orchards disappear.

To sparkle or not to sparkle ?
*that is the **English** question.*

51

May the Almighty bless thee with the blessings of heaven above, and the mountains and the valleys, and the blessings of deep below, with the blessings of Grapes and Apples.

Bless, O Lord, the courage of this Prince, and prosper the work of his hands; and by thy blessing may this land be filled with Apples, with the fruit and dew of heaven, from the top of the ancient mountains, from the Apples of the eternal hills, from the fruits of the earth and its fullness.

Saxon Coronation Benediction

Part Six

Orchards and Apple Trains

Orchards are a halfway house, being neither quite field nor woodland but somewhere in the middle, wonderfully organised, idyllic, but very, very functional. A halfway stage between hunting and gathering, where the useful trees have been left and enough light penetrates to give grazing, though not quite as rich as open ground, but better in a heat-wave. And in the same way that flocks of wild sheep and cattle were slowly tamed and domesticated and cross-bred with selected rams and bulls, so the humble crab apples were slowly domesticated, planted, nurtured and then ranched. In fact these experiments with grafting formed the basis of the new science which we now know as genetic engineering. Indeed crab apples are still planted in hedge rows to help with the pollination of planted orchards.

Every pip from a cider apple will give a hybrid which may or may not produce good fruit. It is only by grafting that you can propagate a certain species, and so get your ordered orchard. Over many generations. The natural landscape we see before us is highly manufactured, beautiful because it is bountiful, a horticultural '*doigt de seigneur*' where man and nature form a healthy alliance.

Indeed while on the subject of pips, apple divinations were, and maybe still are, common, and this in the days before you could consult your stars in the latest teenage magazine, or use the lonely hearts column. One custom in Dorset for young girls to test the fidelity (or was it virility?) of their supposed lover or husband, was to put apple pips on the fire at night when thinking of them. If they burst then the man was full of truth (or was it vigour?) If they died

silently then he was false no good and not worth chasing. Maybe there was more to a pipsqueak than meets the eye, but the dalliance with pips and the pentagram, the pentangle of witchcraft, when cutting an apple open horizontally, is a curious and powerful symbol. Indeed the core of the apple when cut vertically has more than a passing resemblance to female genitalia, if your imagination is fertile that is. Indeed the innocent apple does have, at times, slightly sinister connotations, the poison apple, the bitter crab, even the cider apple, so uninspiring to eat, and yet *the forgotten miracle* is in the juice, the sweetness released, the hidden knowledge, the way ahead, the pleasures of the flesh and senses taken to another plane, a fruity little number, pipped to the post so to speak.

If you love me, pop and fly
If you hate me, lay and die

However to return to divination, things are not always clear-cut, for in Sussex the opposite interpretation was held to be true. In Lancashire a couple would put two pips side by side on a pair of tongs. Left for woman, right for man. If both pips flew off on the same side the two would marry, if in opposite directions they wouldn't. And it wasn't just pips, it was pulp and peel, so passionately did they feel. Often candles were lit and in one hand the girls would hold a mirror while they ate an apple with the other and in the mirror they would see their future husband's face, and in his face their own future... The fated apple... or else a complete peel was thrown over the left shoulder and it would take up the initial of the lucky man or woman. Sometimes this would be done at midnight on Hallowe'en. The variants are enormous but the superstition is firmly embedded in the female consciousness and in the past your future and your economic fate was even more bound up with that of your husband's. But picking the right one is just as tricky today. Apple peel is certainly cheaper than thumbing through a glossy woman's magazine each week, and will fit very neatly into your healthy fat free diet.

But it goes deeper than that, indeed before the adoption of Prince Albert's Germanic Christmas tree, the tradition was to make a kissing bough decorated with ribbons, greenery, apples and candles that would be put up from Christmas Eve till Twelfth Night, the traditional Wassail time... so in a sense it all fits together, the gap between mid winter solstice and the waking of the tree spirits.

But to return to Cider and cidermaking, some say that the art came over with the Normans, in fact it was probably here long before that as the quotes at the beginning show. Legends are notoriously fickle, but they always contain an element of truth, otherwise they would not have survived... .it may well be that the early Irish priests had something to do with it, and certainly the history of Irish Cider has yet to be told this side of the water. Until recently there were strong maritime links between Somerset and Ireland. Even some of the earliest churches on the Somerset coast are dedicated to Irish Saints and an Irish apple the 'Cockagee', which means 'goose shit' in Irish, was reputed to be growing in the Minehead area as late as the 1920's. Apples and bud cuttings are easily transported and survive the damp of a river crossing or boat journey, far better than grain.

In all probability, apples were here long before the Romans, and did play an important part in pre-Christian ritual, but whether the cult of the apple went underground,

to Wales and Ireland when the Roman's came, is difficult to say. It may be, that if it had religious connotations, it was in part actively discouraged by them as they were wine drinkers and imported wine from the continent. So what's new? But the average Roman soldier would have taken what he could get hold of close to hand, as all soldiers do, and if cider was cheaper and hit the right spot, it would have to do. Maybe there was more to Asterix's magic potion than met the eye. With *Pomona* in the background, the Romans would I think have delighted in the English Apple and probably brought their own, no double named *Vespasion*, *Agricola* and *Caesar*.

Interestingly enough the wine which was imported was often sweetened and preserved with lead acetate, a neat little trick which may have led to the downfall of Rome. Certainly archaeologists have an interesting time plotting the lead content in Roman bones and can, I am told, by isolating isotopes identify where the lead came from, and some of it came from distant parts of Europe. Lead also contributed much later to the outbreaks of Devonshire colic in the late eighteenth century, outbreaks that gave cider, at least in the upper circles, a bad name. So always read the label on your Roman wine and late 18th century bottled cider just to check for additives, preservatives and 'E' numbers. Lead acetate has 3 'E's and if you took sufficient quantities of it, your number would certainly be up.

But as always it comes down to climate and local conditions. It just happens that parts of the South West, in the Welsh borders, the Severn and Wye valleys, as well as parts of Brittany and Normandy, are some of the best areas in the world and it is not unnatural that the art of growing apples and making cider should have been there a long time.

Certainly Charlemagne had laws governing the making of cider, though the techniques were a little crude, pulping and beating fruit in a hollowed out trunk and then letting nature take its course... he also decreed that fruit trees should be planted in every town, and this in the year 800. It seems likely that any earlier attempts at making alcohol were not dissimilar...

As far as the machinery is concerned, there were walk-round trough presses for olives in Greek and Roman times, but there is no evidence that Julius Caesar brought them with him, only the infernal siege machines and plans for roads and army camps ready for the supermarkets of today... Interestingly the famous region in Normandy, the *Pays d'Auge*, owes its name to the wooden trough used in the mill called *l'auge*. Spain is not often mentioned but there may well have been influences from the Arab world which crept up from the North African coast. Certainly the old word for still, '*alembic*', comes from there, and then there is the whole Basque region where cider is still their national drink... and if tin was going one way from Cornwall, surely ideas and apples would have gone back the other. Records that have survived are usually church records, which is admirable in itself, but they should not be allowed to rule out earlier suppositions... Indeed whilst on the subject of the church, most of the records show that cider was used extensively to pay off debts, tithes and other dues such as rent and privilege... a kind of currency in other words, a handy little item in a glut year, but then it all came down to storage, and quality, and that depended on apple varieties, soil and secret methods...

Indeed the word *cider,* which has eighteen different variants, may well have come from France or Spain, where it is *cidre* and *sidra*. Certainly the earlier uses of the word in English are closer to these like *Sider*. The earliest apple ever discovered in Europe, came not from England or France, Spain or Italy, but from a peat bog in Northern Ireland and that apple, from Armagh which was mentioned earlier, is being analysed at Oxford by Dr. Juniper at the moment. I bet it wasn't a *Granny Smith*, perhaps it was an *O'Donnell* or a *Michael Collins* or better still... a *Fionn MacCumhail*...

Early remains of dried apples have turned up in tombs in Iraq, Jericho and Turkey. In fact the finger as always points to the fertile crescent, and beyond to Persia and Central Asia. Maybe modern day geneticists will give us the answer and follow the trail back to the remote wild forests of the Tien Shan.

But to give them their due, the Normans, who were, after all, recently converted Vikings with strong beliefs in Odin and other Apple loving Gods tucked up their sleeves, brought over new varieties and monastic orders who had their own ways and means behind walled gardens and closed doors. The word '*mystique*' which comes from the Old French, amply covers this process of transformation or transfiguration. It also carries the right degree of secrecy and wonder, the enigmatic and only partly understood, and yet carrying with it the essence of direct communion with the soul of God. Substitute cider for wine in Holy Communion, add the Green Man, a cider press for the altar, and a few nubile young damsels apple-picking, and you have the old religion, more or less. Tree worship, spirits, fertility and a reverence for nature which is conspicuous by its absence in modern farming techniques, though no doubt organic farming uses *mystique* instead of pesticides to get rid of aphids, leaf curl, rust and sheep scab...

Mystique unfortunately these days sounds more like a male deodorant or an island in the Caribbean frequented by Royal siblings and others. *Mystique*, was a favourite word I believe, with Bertie Bulmer, though there was no '*mystique*' about bulk tankers of apple concentrate from Eastern Europe... though he did fulfil his dream of getting distilling on the map again, and the still is there, for all to see in the Hereford Museum of Cider, and well worth a visit.

But to return to orchards, without which there are no apples, no juice, no cider, no religion. Even the word orchard is much earlier than the Norman invasion of 1066, '*ortgeard*' or '*orceard* ' is recorded in the 9th cent derived probably the latin *'hortus'*, meaning a garden. Formerly it was a garden for herbs and fruit trees and latterly for just fruit trees. The Garden of Eden, the Vale of Evesham, the Vale of Avalon, which some say means the *Isle of Apples*. In fact the Scots Gaelic for apples is *ubhal* the *bh* being pronounced *v* an the word for island is *eilean*. In Irish the word for apple is *ull* and for island is *oilean*. Draw your own conclusions... there was even once a local brew of 'Champagne' Cider called *Avalagne*... which sounds like a new addition to *Neighbours, Brookside or Eastenders*. *Avalagne* was made by Robert Clapp of Baltonsborough near Glastonbury, though this, like much else around Glastonbury, is lost in the Mists of Time... a haze of crystals and joss sticks. But it is a very good apple growing area and many orchards do survive... and if the Glastonbury Festival is anything to go by, cider is still being drunk in vast and profitable quantities. *Pomona* shines sweetly on her devotees, at Midsummer and the rewards are worth waiting for.

Perhaps more down to earth, it is interesting to see that within a Saxon Coronation, apples are mentioned at least three times... and I will repeat the quote from the beginning, which I found in Common Ground's *Apple Games & Customs*, coming as it does, from a nineteenth century book on folklore.

"May the Almighty bless thee with the blessings of heaven above, and the mountains and the valleys, and the blessings of deep below, with the blessings of Grapes and Apples. Bless, O Lord, the courage of this Prince, and prosper the work of his hands; and by thy blessing may this land be filled with Apples, with the fruit and dew of heaven, from the top of the ancient mountains, from the Apples of the eternal hills, from the fruits of the earth and its fullness."

Which apart from being a beautiful evocation of man in the landscape, is a pretty good way of saying that God and Kings have to consider apples as a fairly important ingredient in their existence, and that the fruitfulness and success of one is bound up with the other... It may well be that top grade Cider was used as the libation and drunk in common by those present to seal the ceremony, like ale from the Saxon Horn. It may even be that the tradition of Wassail cups and mugs, the songs and the gathering together in orchards derives in some way from this coronation ceremony, linked in with the wren...

No doubt King Arthur enjoyed a drop of *Avalagne* in the evening as a 'sundowner' in the orchard looking west out over the Somerset levels, with Guinevere, Merlin and Launcelot... Perhaps the orb was a giant cider apple, like a *Catshead* and the Golden Mace for crushing Royal apples in the trough... the Black Rod was for testing the depth left in the Royal barrels... a very tricky operation at the best of times.

For further information about Tree Worship and Kingship it is interesting to consult that great tome *'The Golden Bough'* by Sir James Frazer, a veritable gold mine of information, though he, I think, fails to take on board fully the importance of the English Wassail songs and other customs associated with apple trees, which were still being practised when he was writing his book. Tree spirits, fertility, reverence for ancestors, all are bound up in myth and superstition. Even in Khirgizstan women wanting a child will roll themselves under a solitary apple tree. Is that all I wonder ? In France near Orleans a straw man is paraded through the village and then placed in the oldest apple tree whilst the apples are gathered and then when the apple harvest is over the figure is taken down and either thrown in the water or burnt, the ashes then thrown on the water. The figure is called the great *'mondard'*, a title which applies to the person who picks the first fruit of the season. This is the tree spirit who lies dormant till blossom time...

In the Ardennes on the first sunday in Lent boys and girls would run through the orchards with lighted torches and cry out to the trees.

Sometimes even a cat was burnt as a kind of offering and the shepherd would drive his flocks through the smoke to purify them for the coming year against witchcraft. This seems a little unfair to cats, but no doubt the fire ceremony fitted in with the annual pruning and the bonfires which were no doubt made up from the branches which had been discarded... the livelier the dance round the fire the better the crop.

In Switzerland an apple tree is planted at the birth of a boy, and a pear tree for a girl and the progress of the tree is an indicator of the child's health... Even when my own daughter was born an apple tree started growing of its own accord outside the front door, no doubt from a core thrown there by a previous owner. Both are doing well and respond to pruning...

But then old beliefs in tree spirits and vegetation myths became inevitably bound up with Christianity and the cult of the garden, the orchard and the abbey... Indeed you only have to watch gardening programmes on television to see that the cult is alive and well. A real shame that television wasn't around in the middle ages... *Paradise Gardens* on Channel 4 every Thursday... 8.30pm.

In the twelfth century the Benedictine chronicler William of Malmesbury wrote of the abbey of Thorney in Cambridgeshire, that it was set in *Paradise*, surrounded by green grass and apple bearing trees, i.e. a garden or an orchard in the old sense of the word, and this may well have implied a wall, not just for security but for protection from winds and for warmth being retained on the wall itself. Indeed the word paradise does mean garden, and may well have come from the Persian or Farsi, *pairidaeza*, which means walled or enclosed garden, Iran is only a stone's throw away from the fertile crescent, where, as in Afghanistan, I have seen grapes and apples growing wild in abundance in mountain valleys... The walled garden would be mainly to keep animals and teenagers out...

But in England we have confused the meaning slightly by dropping the word 'earthly', ie the difference between 'earthly' paradise which we can sense, smell, touch and taste and the 'heavenly' paradise about which we can only surmise... such words as 'heaven' we use with gay abandon... *oops* sorry... but the concept of Paradise even gave its name to a famous apple the *Paradise Apple* which was around not only in Worlidge's day but was listed in 1398 in Paris and it comes from, guess where, the Armenian Caucasus, where it was identified in the 19th Cent... For more details and further information see *The Book of Apples* by Joan Morgan and Alison Richards, an excellent tome, with fine illustrations.

But to return to the Monastic Walled gardens, the place of retreat where the temptations and squalor of the real world are kept at arms length. The ideal plan of a Benedictine monastery in the 9th century has two gardens, one for medicinal plants and vegetables and an orchard that is also a cemetery. So you could say that when you died you went to Paradise, which reminds me of a hurdle maker in Ashmore called Cecil Coombes, who, when ever he went to make hurdles in a certain coppice would say with a cheeky smile that he was *'just going to make hurdles in heaven.'*

The idea that the monks were buried in the orchard is a pleasant one, for the orchards would be grazed and never ploughed, so you lay beneath the blossom and even had an apple or two to keep you company, so long as they didn't let the pigs in. Also it saved using other ground which could be useful, like growing vegetables etc...

If only our graveyards were full of apple trees rather than yew and monkey puzzle... imagine it at blossom time, and any apples not picked up could be munched by sheep who best lawnmowers there are, if you can keep them in... And for weddings there would be blossom on hand... Japanese children apparently get their exam results at apple blossom time, and they are told simply that they have either *blossomed* or *not* as the case may be and only get their grades several weeks or months later...

But orchards don't just happen... they have to be planned. *The Great Cyder Bible* in the 17th century was written by John Worlidge, already referred to, and he goes into great detail, as only a scientifically curious gentlemen could at that time. Remember that *Puritanism* and the rigours of Cromwell and the Commonwealth were only just in the past, but Charles II's Restoration was in full swing, as were the Royal Society, the playhouses, the comedies, Pepys's diary and the rapid rise of the orchards of England.

For John Worlidge the ideal spacing was a tree every 20 ft for moderate trees like the *Redstreak*. He allows £5 for the procuring and planting of 100 trees on an acre @ 1/- each, a not inconsiderable sum, as a farmworker's wage even in 1800 was only approx 7/- a week, i.e. each tree was roughly a day's wage which would be nearer £32-£40 at today's rate. But then a tree is £10-£15, the hole has to be dug, the tree staked and guarded, manured etc. so maybe it is not that different...

After seven years the trees will on average yield one bushel each, some more and some less with apples in his day worth 6d the bushel yields 50/- ... At nine or ten years the average may well be two bushels a tree, so you get back annually your original investment plus of course the '*grass keep*' of maybe 20/- a year which covers all the maintenance and pruning etc.

A bushel is equal to four pecks or to put it another way, eight gallons. There are Imperial bushels and Winchester bushels which are slightly less... and used in the U.S. of A. and Canada. Bushels were normally for grain measurement, but could be applied to anything, even girls... bushels of girls, acres of bread... a peck on the cheek.

In a good year when trees are fully mature you might get 500 bushels from the land and the price might be 12d or 18d. The investment pays off very well... in other words you might make £25 in a good year perhaps even more, which in today's terms would be astronomic...

It is the economics of orchards that are of prime importance and it is interesting to note the words of John Clare another great observer of nature, writing nearly 150 years later in his autobiography about a particular Russet tree which lay in his father's garden at Helpstone, near Peterborough.

" *Our cottage was as roomy and comfortable as any of our neighbours and we had it for forty shillings while an old apple tree in the garden generally made the rent... the garden was large for a poor man and my father managed to dig it at night and morning before hours of labour and lost no time. He then did well but the young farmer that succeeded our old landlord raised the rent and the next year made four tenements of the house leaving us a corner of one room on a floor for three guinea a year and a little slip of a garden which was divided into four parts but as my father had been an old tenant he gave him the choice of his share and he retained the old apple tree tho the ground was good for nothing yet the tree befriended us and made shift to make up the greater part of the rent... "*

And later in a letter to J Hessey... "*They are of a particular sort we call them the* **Golden Russet.** *The tree is an old favourite with my father and stood his friend many a year in the days of adversity by producing an abundance of fruit which always met with ready sale and paid his rent. It has borne less latterly till this last season when it produced a great quantity."*

Interestingly enough on the next page is a reference to a farmer called Old Mr Gee, who not only lived in a part of the same house mentioned, and at one time owned it, but lent the young John Clare his first books, almost before he could read. A book on farming called *Robin Hood's Garland* and *The Scotch Rogue*... John Clare talks kindly of the old farmer who, he said, had had a good upbringing and was a decent scholar and always pleased to lend the books. This Mr Gee is, I think, a direct ancestor of my Uncle and God father also called James Crowden, who still lives in Cambridgeshire... His mother was a Miss Gee and it may well be that the Golden Russet mentioned was planted by her family... a curious coincidence... where apples and poetry get intertwined...

So much for John Clare and the *Golden Russet*. It must have been an extraordinary tree and well worth nurturing, like the *Golden Goose*. No wonder John Clare had time to write so much poetry. *Golden Bough* indeed. It is amazing today to think that one family's fortunes should be invested in one tree. How much more an orchard...

Worlidge advises that an orchard facing south-east is to be preferred, for several reasons. Firstly, the easterly winds keep back and check the bud, which means that it does not blossom too early and be caught by unseasonable frosts that can wipe out a whole crop in a single night. The three nights cidermakers most worry about are the May 19, 20, 21. Indeed so serious is the problem of a late frost when you can lose half, or even a whole crop, that folklore has stories in both Devon and Somerset that the Devil did deals with certain brewers of beer, who sold their souls for three nights of late frost... to aggravate the business interests of the cidermakers... In Somerset it is St Dunstan who was allegedly born in Baltonsborough, a cider making village, and in Devon, St Frankan. Indeed those 3 nights in May are known as '*Frankan nights*' to this day... Maybe the threat is not so much the brewing of beer, though that in itself was a threat, but the church itself, which certainly tried its hardest in the nineteenth century to clamp down on the 'heathen' and ungodly practice of cider drinking. It was after all the Reverend Girdlestone who campaigned so vociferously for the farmworkers to be included in the Truck act of 1887, though it is an interesting coincidence that there is a cider apple called *Slack-me-Girdle*, which the Reverend would probably also have heartily disapproved of. Ironically it was also in 1887 that HP Bulmer, the son of a clergyman, seeing a market gap, founded the famous family business. So religion gets in there in all sorts of ways...

There may well have been a political reason as well, in that the brewing of beer could not easily be engaged with on a large scale in a village without recourse to a factory-type brewery and buying in malted barley in competition with the 'Big Boys'... whereas cider making was far more flexible, seasonal and only required a few barrels and access to a press. Or maybe it was not just economics but an attempt either consciously or unconsciously to break up the small close-knit communities that cider drinking encouraged, or was it the other way around ? Indeed it is the tribal thing of communal cider-making which tended to hold the village or farm together... the picking up of the apples and the concern over the making. Indeed there is very much the feeling of a village Parliament where anything and everything is discussed, which only a few cider barns still have.

But to return to Worlidge again, the south eastern orchard gives the plot...

"more sun at the right time of year, i.e. anti-meridian sun, which is esteeemed the best in late summer and autumn... dispersing cold dew early from the child fruits, the air being warmed by the sun all day is sufficient in the evening to preserve and continue the same heat without the sunbeams, and thirdly it affords some shelter from the south- west and west winds, usually prejudicial to the fruit and sometimes very destructive"

"As to shelter, if your ground be moist try poplar and if dry try walnut or ash and a quick hedge of white thorn."

Wise words even today, and they go to show how the familiar English landscape in certain areas of the West Country, is determined more by cider drinking than you might suppose, as well as the economies of orchards and the need to protect the aforesaid orchards, not just from the vagaries of the weather but the unwanted attentions of young cattle who rub bark off and take young shoots. Sheep aren't so bad and after a certain stage sheep not only look good in an orchard but they scavenge the last apples and keep the grass looking like a lawn.

Boys also have to be guarded against and a small item which a friend of mine, Peter Irvine, dug up from the Dorset Archives serves to show the severity with which *scrumping* or stealing apples was taken in the year 1846. The case is taken from the Magistrate's note book in Sturminster Newton. It concerned three boy's ages, are not specified but we assume they are about 12 -13 years old.

"The accused are William Cluett, Job Fudge and Charles Ridout. They were seen in an orchard belonging to William Sweet . He knew the boys well and saw them picking up apples. Charles Ridout was in the adjoining orchard belonging to Mr Rossiter. The apples they were stealing were valued at 3d."

The three boys were obviously up to no good and may well have been arrested, certainly apprehended by the scruff of the neck and sent before the nearest *'beak'*. Tolpuddle and the subsequent transportation of the six *Martyrs* was in 1834, only 12 years before, i.e. in the year of their birth. So their memory must have lingered on. The small village of Tolpuddle, which was then called *Tolpiddle*, lay about a day's walk away. When the young Queen Victoria visited all the *Piddles* became *Puddles* to avoid offence. Even to this day there are still signs about damaging Dorset bridges, the one on Sturminster Bridge from 1832 reads as follows :

DORSET
**ANY PERSON WILFULLY INJURING
ANY PART OF THIS COUNTY BRIDGE
WILL BE GUILTY OF FELONY AND
UPON CONVICTION LIABLE TO BE
TRANSPORTED FOR LIFE
BY THE COURT
T FOOKS**

So the boys must have been in real fear of their lives, or at very least in fear of being transported to New South Wales or Van Dieman's land. When questioned they answered :

William Cluett : What do you say ? : "I SAY NOTHING"
Job Fudge   : What do you say ? : "I SAY NOTHING"
Charles Ridout : What do you say ? : "NOT GUILTY"

The first two boys were fined accordingly :

2/-	Fine
3d	Value of apples
3/6d	Costs

5/9d **Grand Total**

i.e. nearly four days wages for a grown man, a steep fine by any standards... i.e. nearly £100 by today's wage standards. But in those days when people lived by the skin of their teeth and were often forced to steal to survive, it must have been a bitter blow to their families... they didn't even get to keep the apples... Charles Ridout got off *'scott'* free... All three surnames are, as it turns out, well known in the area even today...

Sometimes stolen apples were called *'shoulderings'* as they were carried home in a sack on the shoulder. A good friend of mine in Shaftesbury, who was brought up in the Sturminster area, John Cluett, says that that it couldn't possibly have been a relation of his caught *scrumping*, as he and his family were *'far too respectable'*. It must have been those other *Cluetts*, the *Marnhull Cluetts* he said, with a twinkle in his eye.

But John likes his cider, all the same, and as he says there's nothing better to wash down bread and cheese. As to language, John was given the strap at school in the thirties for using dialect words, which were in fact pure Anglo-Saxon, and that at the same time as Anglo-Saxon was being taught as part of the first year English course in Oxford, without perhaps realising that it was still alive and well and kicking in the Sturminster area. John's education left him *'black and blue'*, and no doubt the same forces that drove out cider drinking wanted to purify the language of village youths. John still uses a thick layer of dialect morning, noon and night, and his recitation of William Barnes is second to none... *'Barnes I have seen converted'* as he says. Many of the words he uses are archaic, like *'thicky'* for that one, *'zull'* for plough and *'plow'* for wagon. Indeed the Dorset farmworkers meal times were *dewbit, breakfast, nuncheon, cruncheon, nammet, crammit and supper,* though it is unlikely they would have had enough food for all seven. Cider no doubt would have been taken at all times... though on some farms *nammet* is the first morning break at about nine-thirty.

Often the cider was safer than water... It had after all been drawn up the tree, preserved in the apples, had the lifeblood squeezed out of it, and then fermented, and then strained. Nothing wrong with cider when cholera and typhoid lurked about...

John still likes a drop brought to his back door. Indeed he says that when he was a boy, " Dennis Holloway's father, a farmer near Stalbridge, always advertised for workers with the words *'House and Good Cider'* added and he had a queue

stretching to Dorchester. And *that* on the front page of *'The Western Gazette'*, and that 50 years after cider was officially banned as truck." But as John says, "it must have been *'damn good cider'*... and they worked hard for it too, pitching sheaves up onto the wagon." Something you don't see very often these days, a whole field stitched up for thatching straw, but what a sight it is when you do see it. "And they told you to keep the horse moving and then on the rick they pitched every one just right, *'tread 'em in the middle'* they used to say and you never had to alter a single one... and *that* rick stayed tight till thrashing."

John also remembers not only certain cider farms and small cider factories but a farm where you could get what they called *cider wine,* which he is sure was *cider brandy...* He was doing a butcher's round at the time during the war, but the driver was an ex-policeman, and warned the young John Cluett, *'not to touch any of that cider wine...'*

" The place was near Fifehead Neville and had a certain reputation, and when talking about it they would always chuckle and give you a knowing look. And I am sure it was the cider brandy, it weren't just extra sugar, you couldn't get the sugar during the war see, it must have been a little extra on a stove, and a bit of know how, producing a bit of *cow medicine,* but you weren't supposed to know... That was Goddards... you see Geoff Peck went with the daughter there and he had a basin full one night and then rode his bike back towards Sturminster, but he came off, a real cropper, and lay in the road for hours before anyone came to pick him up, you see it was late at night and cars were few and far between, and he did himself a bit of an injury..."

John Cluett also remembers when he worked on the railways at Sturminster Newton, the cider apple trains came up from Hamworthy, near Poole, every autumn :

"Great steel coal trucks that we'd sent down in the morning, now filled up with French apples just off the dock and bound for *Bulmers* at Hereford, with French apples from Normandy. They would always come up at about half past ten at night and then go through to Bath and Bristol... arriving in Hereford in the morning. Maybe forty or fifty wagons at a time and fresh from France. Maybe every night for a week or ten days. The smell on a cold night was wonderful and lingered on for ten minutes or more, the scent of French apples on their way to Hereford through the night, maybe ten tons to a truck that would be four or five hundred tons of apples on the move at one go. Marvellous really when you think about it, and at night better than nuclear waste, and they did it one go to Bath without refuelling or watering, all steam you see, though I do wonder how well they had washed out the coal trucks... maybe that's how they got that deep colour into their cider... and that went on every autumn in the late fifties till about 1963."

John Cluett's career on the railways was as Porter *Second Class* which isn't a reference to the local beer, and Signalman *Fourth Grade*... Porter *First Class* sat inside in the warmth of the office and did paper work.

Not surprisingly cider went into a bit of a siding in Dorset after the Second War and by 1980 there were only a few producers left. My brother and I poked our noses into a cider factory at Shillingstone which had belonged to Lujen Robins and it was full of the barrels and equipment and a large number of old bicycles, and cobwebs galore. But it was sold off and the contents scattered to the four winds. Walking in there was extraordinary, it had been closed down fifteen or twenty years but the atmosphere lingered on. This was on the west bank of the River Stour and thus sheltered from the south-west winds. Okeford Fitzpaine was another cider village, and Fiddleford. They were solid orchard areas and must have produced a fair drop in their time and they could get it on the train you see.

But there were no big firm like *Taunton Cider, Coates, Whiteways* or *Bulmers*, otherwise it would have been a very different story. But as John Cluett says you can't have *'damn*

good cider' without a *'damn good orchard'* and most of them's *'all to cock these days, run down and scrabbity'*. At least the thatcher in Durweston kept on making cider after we left... Tradition dies hard, but nothing I fear will ever touch the smell of those apples passing through the darkened Dorset and Somerset countryside bound for Hereford with a good head of steam and the sound of the engine rippling through the night...

"Under a full moon, scent from France –
A river of apples on the silver rails..."

There is a legend that at the time of the Roman invasion some of the inhabitants of Britain fled to the West, while others crossed the channel to Armorica, now known as Brittany. With them they took their apple trees... later they were followed by St Brieuc and his monks. In the sixth century St Teuilic of Wales visited Normandy and with the help of Bishop Sampson, planted an extensive orchard - this led according to tradition to the first cidermaking in those parts.

The remains of this orchard the *Arboretum Teliavi et Sampsonis* were still to be seen in the 12th Cent...

from *Cidermaking* by Pollard & Beech 1957

There are references to cider in Spain in the 4th Cent.

Walter Minchinton 1975

Part Seven

John Worlidge and Hard Graft

But there is far more to orchard husbandry than meets the eye, and to make what John Cluett calls a *'damn good orchard'* requires not only good soils, good inclination, good species, good spacing and good pruning but a lifetime's dedication. It is an art and a science and even a religion all rolled into one, a point made time and time again by John Worlidge, and much of what he said in 1678 holds true today. And very often what is not visible is just as important as that which is visible, i.e. the soils which may have taken thousand of years to form and mature.

"As to soils, choose a good warm light rye land, for the heavier colder moister wheat land is not so good. A firm and strong land is better for winter and lasting fruit, the more it inclines to reddness the better. If the ground be hot, dry, shallow, or barren ridges, are best."

And indeed you can see this in old orchards, the slight ridge and furrow in the evening light, or in the early morning when my brother would say *'the shadows of cow pats are very long'*. But in some areas Worlidge even advocates irrigation, a concept now used to a much wider extent in agriculture generally.

"Water can be used in irrigation channels as with water meadows, or if that is not available, chalk, marle or clay laid on the ground will make the ground very rich. If the ground be cold moist and spewy you can dig trenches to try and drain it and in the bottom place alderfrith or faggots some say beech lasts longest... And if your ground be cold clay, lighten it with sand and dung and keep the ground annually ploughed. And lastly if the land be subject to flooding this is a good sign for the land will improve so long as the floods recede quickly."

The choice of good rye land is also included in a long and interesting poem written in 1708 by John Phillips, extolling the virtues of cider and including finely described details of certain key operations.

"But, Farmer, look, where full eared sheaves of Rye
Grow wavy on the Tilth, that soil select
For Apples; thence thy Industry shall gain
Tenfold Reward ... thy Press with purest Juice
Shall flow..."

Perhaps it is no coincidence that the postal address for the Hereford Cider Museum is 21 *Ryelands* St... Hereford.

As to the propagation of fruit trees, Worlidge devotes no less than forty seven pages to this most esteemed of arts.

" There is no fruit tree in this whole Isle of Great Britain that is so universal as the apple tree; there being but few places and but little land wherein it delighteth not ; hardly any place so cold or so moist, hot or dry, but will thrive and bear fruit"

To understand the cider apple you have to understand grafting and you need good grafting stock. For Worlidge it is either crab stock, wilding stock or the *Paradise Apple*, already mentioned.

A good, strong, hardy fast growing root stock is the crab which...

"not only preserves but quickens and enlivens the guts of any delicate apple. But if the apple you intend to propagate be over-tart, then sweeten it on a Gennet Moyle of Wilding stock"

"You may obtain crabstocks out of the woods and hedgerows and plant them in the places where you intend they shall stand. The crabstock also thrives best when removed from a cold, dry hilly land to a warm and fertile soil."

Just like bringing sheep down from the hill... to graze in the fertile valleys. They do ever so well, even the old ones with no teeth... just like going to the south of France for a holiday in the autumn.

Worlidge divides the apple trees into three varieties which hold good today... Firstly, early cider, like *Morgan Sweet*, Secondly main batch cider, *"rich, oily, spicey, highly relished cider also long lasting and Thirdly such as will provide useful fruit for the table but will make very pleasant and acceptable cider.'*

Of the first he mentions the *Codlin* and the *Gennet Moyle*. Of the second, his favourite and much loved Redstreak from Herefordshire of which there are several sorts, and bred and made popular by Mr Scudamore himself who introduced the variety in the 1630's.

The *Redstreak* has his overall approval for several reasons. First because it *"yields the best of British drink..."* Second because the fruit is *"harsh and unpleasant, not tempting the palates of lewd persons... Thirdly the tree thrives in mean land... Fourthly it is a constant bearer being a wilding enduring during the severity of sharp springs sometimes destructive to those that are more tender... Fifthly the tree bears in a few years after*

grafting... Sixthly the tree is low and humble and so more can be planted to the acre... Seventhly the lowness of the trees prevents the sharp winds of the spring and the fruit of them are not apt to be blown off in autumn and Eighthly the fruit exceed all the fruit in the kitchen while it lasts..."

Indeed so popular was this apple and held in so high esteem that J Phillips has this to say about it.

"Let every Tree in every Garden own
The **Redstreak** *as supreme; whose pulpous fruit*
With Gold irradiate and Vermillion shines...
... Heav'n's sweetest blessing, Hail
Be thou the copious Matter of my Song
And thy choice Nectar, on which always waits
Laughter, and Sport, and care beguiling Wit,
And Friendship, chief Delight of Human Life"

It is as if the philosophy of living, and good living at that, is embodied in the apple itself, which extols the virtue of this drink over those of foreign countries, which may have more to do with economics, propaganda, advertising, self-promotion, wars and an anti-European feeling not unknown even today... For example here is the proud landowner serving his best *cyder* to foreign visitors who have no inkling that it is made within spitting distance of the farmer's back door.

"Some cyders have by Art, or Age unlearn'd
Their genuine relish, and of sundry Vines
Assumed the flavour; one sort counterfeits
The Spanish Product; this, to Gauls has seem'd.
The sparkling nectar of **Champaigne:** *with that,*
A German oft has swill'd his Throat, and sworn,
Deluded that Imperial Rhine bestow'd
The Generous Rummer, whilst the Owner pleas'd

You can almost hear the Herefordshire farmer chuckling even now, this pride in his own native soil. The products of their labours and experimentation, not only rivals wine but exceeds it in value and even breeds an affectionate John Bull type of rampant nationalism, which encourages the farmer to seek more carefully native products and native markets, as valid today as it was then. Perhaps today, even more so, the growth of the Organic Market, the subtleties of regional and *landscape produce*. Individuality within the complexity of the apple, which led to a call for organic brand loyalty even in 1708...

"Meanwhile wilt not Thou reject
Thy Native Liquors : Lo for Thee my Mill
Now grinds choice Apples, and the British Vats
O'erflow with generous cider..."

And as to other varieties, the *Golden Pippin* is mentioned, as is the *Westbury apple* from near Petersfield, so called *"from the Villa where the old tree stood that that yielded grafts to its neighbours. they are tough and may yet be kept till midsummer following"*

Apples that could keep were at a premium... another apple mentioned not unlike the Westbury is the *'Deux Ans'* because it will keep for two years and has ' *a clean rind not attacked any canker'*. These later apples should not be turned into cider till at least December. Other apples mentioned are *Elliot, Stoken Apple, Musts and Fillets.*

In this day and age, of freeze-dried and chilled foods we are not really able to experience the problems or indeed the thrills of finding an apple that will keep well and will taste good even after a year. It was after all the Vikings who first got to Greenland and then went south to get to the rest of Canada and possibly even into what is now known as America. Was the apple there before Columbus ? And if so how did it get there ?

Such rare genetic species that would last two years till at their peak could yet outwit the supermarket forces which have dictated that everything must be in prime condition within a day or two of picking, then flown around the world three times and still be almost tasteless... It is perhaps a symptom of our times that appearances count for more than reality, perhaps after all flavour might just have something to do with it...

If only we kept our fruit well and bred our orchards accordingly and redeveloped the local taste... a loyalty to regions which farmer's markets are now starting to tap into very successfully. A Market that the W.I. never left, though even they might have to consider updating their procedures where you have by tradition, to queue three times for something. First to 'ear mark' whatever it is you want at that particular stand, then it is put to one side, submerged, among a flurry of bags and baskets, and you are given a ticket. At this stage you feel important, then you go round queuing at each stall in the same manner, collecting tickets, then you go and pay at another long queue where everything is very clearly and carefully marked up in the books. Then you queue again to get your produce back and you may well have already queued a fourth time to simply get into the hall in the first place. Perhaps it is a hang over from women bonding together during the war with food rationing. But the frustration of seeing what you have waited for, being snatched from under your nose, by a little old lady who has just very successfully queue barged in front of you, can take several years off your life.

But to return to John Worlidge and apples... Of the third class, there are *Pippins and Permains* but of all the table fruit *Gilliflower and Marigold Apple and Kate Apple and Onion*

Apple are to be preferred. *The Golden Rennet, Harvey Apple and Queening* are good cider apples.

As to pears he mentions *Choakie* pears of Worcestershire, the *Horse Pear, Bareland pear and Bosbury pear*. Plums damsons, cherries, gooseberries, currants and raisins are also mentioned for liquor, from which we deduce that the home-made wine industry was flourishing then. Indeed without television, one's creative ingenuity knew no bounds, and the price of good wine being what it was then, every Englishman and woman scoured the hedgerows and experimented. *Deep down you knew it made sense.*

Then again, husbandry was not just sheep, corn, cattle and turnips. There was an air of optimism, Renaissance man with a pruning knife in one pocket and slim volume of the classical poets in the other. It was an age of expansion on the soil before the age of capitalism and industry dug deep into rural parts and sucked the workforce from the land. That's another story, but it was *that* workforce that later drunk the vast quantities of cider that kept the nineteenth and even early twentieth century orchards and entrepreneur farmers going...

Hard graft is where it's at, and for grafting you needed a sharp curved knife and green fingers, the skill, the knack that makes all this possible. You choose the root stock and then the bud of the tree you wish to propagate or in the words of John Worlidge you choose :

"the best bearing trees and from such boughs or sprigs that are most apt to bear, the spring before its bearing year, if it be a tree that (as many usually do) bears every other year."

Which, although a mouthful, is logical, for most orchards are on a two year cycle. You always have the '*on*' year and the '*off*' year, the trick being to gauge it just right, with your grafting, but also with your cider sales, so that you don't run out of cider in the summer after the '*off*' year... rationing

even for regular customers has been known, but is always accompanied by much mumbling, grunting, heaving of opinions, and turgid shakes of the head. But to return to grafting :

" as for size let them be short, with two or three eyes or buds at most and those nearer together, the better. Grafts are usually cut a little below the knot or joint of the last year's growth because the wood is there hard, and the rind thick, to shoulder well into the stock."

"When once the leaf is wholly off, and before the tree begins to bud again, grafts then may be kept until the spring or grafting time, the ends being stuck into the ground and transported or carried to any remote place. If ends be stuck in clay or a turnip or they be bound up in green moss, or being wrapped in oiled waxen leather, the intent being to keep them cool and from exsiccating winds; for in frosty and windy weather trees being laid in a cellar, or such places are preserved when otherwise exposed to the winds though much more cold, are destroyed."

Keeping your grafts in good condition is essential and required as much skill as keeping potatoes from frost damage.

"March is the best month for grafting apples milde open weather is best and most propitious for this work. Yet observe that a graft sometimes before cut and stuck in the ground and then grafted at the rising of the sap, takes better than those that are grafted so soon as cut."

Here, as on other occasions, John Worlidge excels himself with fine detail and obviously has a keen interest but on the subject of sap rising, a not uninteresting phenomenon even today, and not just in trees either, he opens up and waxes lyrical...

"But the more general rising of the sap is upon the approaching of the sun into our northern hemisphere, opening the pores of the earth, and which by its vital and attractive heat and influence, dissolves the bonds of that spirit of the World that flowes into all vegetables, and from them into animals, to the maintaining of that Universal Harmony that is in the processes of nature."

The language quite overtakes him and with some gusto... A laudable and accurate description. Such a concept of Universal Harmony is sadly lacking today, though some of the more enlightened strive towards it. Even in Worlidge's day although there was perceived to be Universal Harmony in Nature, as God or the Monarch intended, such questions as how Universal Harmony should regard such pithy problems as religious tolerance, slavery and women's rights, were as yet only surfacing. The Monmouth Rebellion was still nearly a decade in the offing when John Worlidge wrote his Treatise, but like many of his contemporaries he sought inspiration and even guidance from the Classics, and here indicates that the grafting of trees is nothing new, as Virgil mentions...

> *"The oft without impairing we may see*
> *The boughs of one graff'd in another tree."*

As to grafting itself, the science and skill, Worlidge covers this in great detail which is well worth repeating and as always in his own words...

"The most common and as yet may be supposed ancient way, is the grafting in the stock, and that is either by cleaving the stock, or grafting in the rind, or by whip grafting."

"Grafting in the cleft, is to cut off the stock at a smooth place at the height you intend and if the stock be small, from one to three inches diameter, then cleave it that the slit be on the smoothest side of the stock, and sit your graft, shouldering it at the joint or bud, joining the insides of the rinds exactly

The inconvenience this manner of grafting is subject to, is, that the stock being slit, the rind is apt to get in and decay the stock. Therefore caution must be used not only the first year but until the head of the stock be covered to defend it from wet by good luteing of it or by wax which is best."

Luteing is a tenacious clay which will bind the graft, the word deriving from the Latin *lutus,* for mud.

But as with most delicate operations, size matters... *"if the stock exceed three inches diameter or thereabouts, the best way is to graft the rind or bark which is done with a wedge made of ivory, box or other hard wood, made of a flat half round form tapering to a point, and force the same in between the rind and the stock until you have made a passage wide enough for the graft, the end whereof must be cut after the same form with the rind peeled off, preserving on, as much of the inner rind as you can and making the graft to shoulder well on the stock."*

The inconvenience of this method is that they usually make large shoots the first year which *"in case the wind happen to blow strongly on the opposite side of the stock, where the graft is, is commonly broken off, having as yet no other hold than in the rind... To prevent this you must nip off with your nails those that aspire too high and abate some of the broader leaves which like sails give the wind advantage. Next year the shoots will spread better..."*

Even John Phillips makes a fine description of grafting :

> *"Let Art correct thy Breed: from Parent Bough*
> *A Cyon meetly sever; after, force*
> *A way into the Crabstock's close wrought Grain*

By Wedges, and within the living Wound
Enclose the Foster Twig ; nor over-nice
Refuse with one's own Hands around to spread
The binding Clay; Ere-long their differing veins
Unite, and kindly Nourishment convey
To the new pupil...'

A rare thing perhaps, such beauty describing a lowly yet important rural task, and like the grafts themselves, language has its own tender shoots on native rootstocks that either take or not as the case maybe... words become fused from other cultures and even the meaning of words changes over time, words ripen and hybrids form. Such is slang and dialect which soon becomes absorbed in unusual company.

But to return to Worlidge and his almost inexhaustible supply of information and the pithy question of size...

"If the stock be under an inch in diameter, then the best way is to whip on the graft, that is to say if the stock be bigger than the graft, then cut the stock off at the smoothest place and a little sloping. Some place the graft to the upper side of the slope, some to the lower, which is the better way that the rind or bark may cover the sooner, and which side it ever so be, the rind must be pared away beginning easily, and so deeper upwards till you cut to the wood at the top, then pare the end of the graft accordingly with a full and broad shoulder to rest on top of the stock, and fit it aptly to the stock, and bind it on with hemp or yarn, basse or such like."

Basse being the inner bark of lime or linden or any palm fibre.

"But if the graft and stock be near of size, then cut the graft aslope and end the stock likewise and bind them together rind to rind. This is the best way to graft, the inconveniences that attend both the other being prevented."

A real and rich mouthful but so delicately and accurately described that even the simplest amateur could with care follow these instructions to the letter even three hundred years later.

Until recently the grafters in prime orchards were men much revered like prize-winning shepherds, for in their skill and art of pruning also lay the future of the orchard and the future of the owner. For in the hands of an expert an orchard could be encouraged and coaxed to double and sometimes triple its yields.

But the expert advice does not stop there... for there is the art of transplanting trees, an operation where Worlidge draws inspiration from the French poets about planting new dwarf species and the different skills required in husbanding them. Remember this is still 1678...

"In open plains on which the warm sun shines
there let your Tree aspire. In grounds enclosed
let a dwarf-race of Fruit trees be disposed
Whose boughs are round and short; not bodies tall."

Indeed these dwarf varieties must have been new for Worlidge and not without his approval, for he advises :

"Let no one think it is a disparagement to our nation, to imitate the excellencies of any others, nor think that our forefathers were so wise, as to know all things."

"Every race of mankind, and every age endeavouring to improve the Actions of the former do assuredly discover something better than what was before, or at least bring into practice that which they concealed."

Apt words for the Age of Discovery, advocating an Open Mind in all matters, whilst not taking everything as Gospel. You can smell the Age of Optimism in the reign of Charles

II, the return of men, frightened for their lives after the horrors of the Civil War and the restrictions of the Puritan and Commonwealth Realm... There had to be some cause for optimism, the Greenwich Observatory, the new found centre of the timely world which, in Worlidge's case may be, not in Greenwich, but in Hereford itself. Gravity and the *Newton Wonder*, on the back burner, the power of terrestrial mathematics, learning by degrees in Cambridge, the art and science of cooking, apples, heavenly orbs, which might as well be seen on display rather than hid beneath Puritan cloth... a new found sensuousness that found its way not just onto the stage.

Worlidge also draws a quick hint from none other than Virgil transplanting trees from the nursery by marking with chalk the orientation, the North, South, East, and West inclinations on the bark so that when replanted these can be replicated in the orchard so as not to disrupt the trees inner growth patterns...

"And having thus marked your tree, take them up with as large Roots as you can, especially the spreading roots. Therefore it is best to keep the spade from coming too near to the tree... endeavour to raise as much earth as you can with the tree, but if it be to carry it far, shake it off."

Wise words, why indeed carry too much soil...

"In Planting of your tree abate the downright roots, leaving those that spread, for it is observed, that the more the root spreads, the more the branches, tall trees usually extending their roots deepest."

Or as Virgil would have it:

"How much to heaven her spreading branches shoot
So much towards hell extends her fixed root."

"Of those roots you leave, prune the ends by cutting them like under a hind's root on the under side, they will put forth new roots better. In case trees have lain too long, settle in the bottoms of pools and ditches or rotten vegetables or burnt earth or anything that will either mend or alter the ground that is proper for your trees. Fill to such a convenient height that you may plant your tree on top of it and then add good mold about the root and dilute it with water as before directed, then level earth about the tree so that it may not be too high to injure the bark..."

"after you have placed your tree to your mind and covered the roots with good natural mold then take a wheel barrow full of street dirt or dirt tempered by the tramplings of cattel ,most especially hogs, and cover the loose ground around the tree and pat it smooth with the back of your spade, plaister like inclining towards the tree; this may be laid two or three inches thick and in breadth two or three feet round the tree, by which means the loose earth will remain moist and weeds prevented from too sudden growth."

It is after all good husbandry, as Alan Titchmarsh would, I think, acknowledge. But it is the detail and the manure, the getting it just right, which will give your young trees the best start in life... Often with a lamb an extra bit of nurturing at the beginning will pay dividends later in life... indeed in the *moluccas* fruit trees are even married one to the other and at blossom time treated like pregnant women. Their owners believe that at a certain time it is critical while the fruit sets, which it is, and these beliefs which on one level seem naive, are in fact steeped not only in ancient tradition, but perhaps more importantly show a deep respect for the tree itself, the natural world and the sense of gratitude to the trees, without which their lives would be poorer.

Very often the function of superstition is to engender that

respect in every generation, where it might be lacking. Our own modern consumer high-tech world is sadly lacking in tradition but new interest in the environment and the spiritual side of nature and the awareness of the 'self' within, are all part of the careful balancing act we have with nature. But Worlidge and his experimenters were after quantity and quality... so the spacing and layout of an orchard was paramount.

They were trying to get the best out of their soil just as much as farmers are today, but with the top end of the fine wine and drinks market in mind. The 'A's and ' B' s of their day... Dukes, Duchesses, Judges and Admirals. Though if Judge Jeffreys had drunk more *cyder* he would probably not have had such bad kidney stones or gout, indeed he may not have had a kidney stone at all, and the harsh judgements he doled out for the survivors of the Monmouth Rebellion might have been ameliorated somewhat...

" *Bring in ye next prisoner... let us see his Rascally face*"
"*Don't waste ye Court's Time by pleading ye Innocence*"
"*The love of Fair Play and Justice...*
...is in the very marrow of my bones"

Even John Philips writing in 1708, only twenty years after Sedgemoor mentions...

"*Civil Broils fermenting from Social cups...*
Atheist rebels, bent to Ill
With seeming sanctity and cover'd Fraud"

"*Yet was the Cyder-land unstained with Guilt*
The Cyder-land, Obsequious still to thrones
Abhorr'd such base disloyal Deeds and all
Her Pruning hooks extended into Swords
Undaunted to assert the trampled rights
Of Monarchy."

At first I thought this referred to The Battle of Sedgemoor in 1685, but it is far more likely to refer to the Civil War and Royalist sympathies in Hereford and Worcester, which under Cromwell's Dictatorship :

"*Long groan'd beneath*
Tyrannic Sway, 'till fair-revolving Years
Our exil'd Kings, and Liberty restor'd
Now we exult by mighty ANNA's Care
While She to foreign Realm's
Sends forth her dreadful Legions."

No doubt referring to the exploits of the John Churchill, the First Duke of Marlborough, let loose in the Low Countries. But to return from politics and strife to the world of orchards, Worlidge has this to say about that all important science, spacing :

"*As for the distance of Trees, it ought to be according to the nature of the tree and the soil. If it be a large spreading tree and a rich soil, forty foot is a good distance. If a Redstreak, or a such like dwarfish short lived tree, twenty foot is enough between them.*"
"*Always observe that the greater the distance, the better the sun meliorates the fruit and if the ground be good, the better do the trees thrive, and the poorer the ground is, the trees being thick, the better they shadow it, the moor the trees do prosper...*"

So in a sense it is like human beings, get the spacing right and nature does the rest, often it is the overcrowding of people in cities that leads to all kinds of trouble, but space them too far apart and they fade away for lack of company. Yet monoculture is not always a good thing either, and for the pollination of orchards, species are often mixed row by row to increase the yield... Bees are also an important feature not lost on John Worlidge, who not only incorporates a whole section on Bees and Bee keeping at the end of his treatise, but also advocates inter-cropping or inter-planting as we would know it today...

"And if you design a plantation of many sorts of fruits in one lot, then may you plant your apples and pears the further apart and between them or in subordinate rows you may plant cherry trees and such like, and next unto them filberts currants, gooseberries Etc. so that if ever the greater trees spread far by that time the lesser may have decayed; if those do not, those may be renewed that no part of the plot may be fruitless."

Wise man. Inter-planting will reduce the risk of disease wiping out any one crop and the frost likewise, for the apple trees will not all blossom or bud at the same time. In a sense it is a game of chance and a gamble, but a calculated gamble...

"as for pruning ... be cautious of cutting small sprigs which are the more apt to bear fruit, it being usual for ignorant planters to beautify their trees by taking of those superfluous branches as they term them wherby they deprive themselves of the fruit."

Pruning is an art in itself and the pruner must have an understanding of how the tree works, each species having slightly differing characteristics. Leave enough space in the middle to throw your hat through, and leave the right shoots, to increase the chances of budding. Also to prune at the right time of year... before the sap is risen...

In characteristic style John Worlidge ends this tremendous section with a small mention of Swine... which has their own peculiar interest and advantage...

"Swine which are pernicious to all gardens, yet are profitable in an orchard. Therefore after your trees have gained strength

enough to bear the rubbing of these cattel, you may keep your swine in your orchard all the winter season, unringed, by which means you orchard will not only be thoroughly diggd, but enriched by the excrements of those diggers. In spring you may level it out again, which will exceedingly conduce the fertility of your plantation.

Thus swine which never were accountable useful whilst alive, may now become the best improvers of your orchards: repine not at the loss of your grass that will not be so much prejudiced as your fruit ameliorated..."

So in Worlidge's eyes, pigs win over sheep. Just imagine it pigs finished off on pomace, then air dried bacon, *Palma* ham of the orchards yet again, or smoked on apple wood or even the combination of pork and apple sauce, a neat mixture not unknown today. But the orchards must have been pretty muddy in a wet winter and some damage to roots must have taken place...

The orchard is thus worthy of major treatise, words scientific and poetic, French and even Latin, extolling the virtues of grafting, and inter-planting spacing. These all make the orchard a special place on the farm and usually not too distant from the farmhouse, hence a likely haunt for farmer's daughters who wish for piece and quiet... A chance to be entertained away from the watchful eye of father... and if the farmer has hacked down this most beautiful of forests because it does not agree with his choice of combine harvester, or European grant, then it is a sad loss, for generations yet to come... One old Norwegian farmer I knew who was living at Gutch Common near Shaftesbury and always ploughed with horses, Siegvart Godeseth, planted a cherry orchard in his last years so that his grand children could play in it and he could hear their voices... and that after a hard life on the land. It is perhaps through trees, and orchards in particular that we convey our sense of permanence in an otherwise largely impermanent world, and at the same time there is blossom, fruit, juice, beverage even spirit, and firewood...

We should fight to save our orchards and save the fuel that speeds the apple, out of season, half way round the world, for we have grown lazy in our lofts and have not the time or the energy to grow and preserve that which is closest to our hearts.

For convenience read sloth, or lack of time, our lives are so speeded up it is a miracle that we have time to eat and register that we are actually alive and well and part of a living world that is always changing. At least in an orchard you have time to stop and stare and hopefully to wonder at the complexity of nature.

The orchard is God's garden, the paradise that we seek in our minds, and don't forget the birds and the bees, the robin and the wrens and the tom tits, a hive of activity, the tree spirits, the Celtic spirits that we have all but lost over the years. Fluid images that somehow mirror our more subtle beliefs in matters which also affect not just our own well being, but hat of those around us. Life without apples and cider may well have meant no life at all, and the consumption of apples may well have prevented ailments which if unchecked could have led to debilitating and even fatal diseases like scurvy on land and sea...

The apple is an easily transported item and keeps better than almost any other fruit... time indeed to revive its fortunes within these shores, and to have the same diversity and quality on our supermarket shelves, as we have with now have with beer and cheese and bread...

Maybe the national sentiments are not out of place at all... they just need resurrecting like the wren on the back of the farthing... Orchards have their own pace and rhythm and language, and even in the rich depths of Greek mythology... the competition for favours, good looks, beauty, intelligence and cunning, a bit of wooden horse trading and form. Wasn't it an apple that started the Trojan wars... a *Spartan* perhaps or a *Helen of Troy* ?

It's all there for the picking...

For then you may, after due fermentation, extract Spirits, vulgarly called *Brandy*, in great plenty, and very excellent quick and burning...

John Worlidge 1678

Duties payable for all *Cyder and Perry* : the sum of four shillings for every hogshead... All and every distiller that shall receive any quantity of *Cyder or Perry* into his, her or their Custody shall give notice in writing to the proper Officer whose Survey any such Distiller shall reside, Forty Eight hours before he, she or they shall begin to put any Quantity of the same into any Still or Stills to be drawn into low Wines or Spirits...

An Act of Parliament for continuing and granting to his Majesty certain Duties upon *Malt, Mum, Cyder and Perry*. 1759

Part Eight

Distilling - The Spiritual Side

Planting and tending the orchard is one thing, then there is harvesting, the pressing, the fermentation, the storage the blending - the transition from blossom to apple to juice to cider. And then there is the secret mysterious part, the transfiguration, the resurrection, the Holy Ghost, the spirit that evaporates and condenses as perfect as nectar, *avant garde mystique,* ardent and sensuous, clear and aromatic. like the forbidden fruit, that has been smuggled out from the Garden of Eden. The tree of knowledge, first bite of the apple, naked truth yielded from the serpent coils of the copper pipe and swan-necked curves lovingly polished and warmed to perfection; the orchard's wake, tickled and cajoled into life, ingenuity tinged with a little daring and coaxing, tempting the liquor from its former self, a slight cheekiness not unknown in poaching circles; the Spirit of the Gods brought to earth as if by magic, the allure of secret skills passed on under cover of darkness...

The list is endless, but the message is the same. Distilling is one of nature's finest kept secrets, and with the connivance of the Government Customs and Excise would like to keep it that way. They imagine somehow that they have a monopoly on taxing nature's gift, in the same way that we are charged for water from the heavens, and in the same way that salmon are free agents in the ocean of life, until they come within a few feet of a be-whiskered Colonel in tweeds. Only then does the legality of certain operations come into question.

Centuries of dogged obedience and Puritan beliefs have left their trace and yet we still hanker after the nomadic life, the gipsy, the poacher, the traveller, the green man, the under-dog defying authority, the smuggler, the man in the backwoods brewing up lethal concoctions... Moonshining is in fact quite simple and just requires the source liquid, cider, beer, plum wine or whatever, to be brought up to the magical temperature of 78^0C and to hold it just above that for as long as it takes to drive the alcohol off rather than the water, which of course all comes off at 100^0C as steam. And then the real trick is to devise some mechanism for collecting the vapour without it disappearing or becoming saturated again. One's earliest chemistry lessons dwell on the subject of Specific Vapour Pressure, latent heat of evaporation, boiling points etc. etc. which although unimaginably boring at the time and appeared to have no significance whatsoever, apart from filling up the long hours between meals and endless games of rugby, all of a sudden become of extreme importance and interest, as if somehow your life and well being might depend on it.

With the simplest systems a second vessel is placed above the main vessel, and this second vessel is kept cool with water, its bottom surface is where the liquor or distillate condenses and beneath it is placed a dish to collect the drips of alcohol as they form. The dish is emptied every so often and the water at the top is changed to keep it cool. This is a basic but effective method.

It is used throughout the world and I have seen it used very effectively in the depths of the Himalaya using yak dung to fuel the fire, the Buddhists of Ladakh being given special dispensation from Delhi to distil in their own homes, though the rest of India was dry, a much admired privilege during Mrs Ghandi's emergency. The extreme conditions of cold being a more important factor than the state religions of Islam and Hinduism which both frown upon anything to do with spirits, though India itself blossoms with distilleries and spiritual advice. The secret is to keep the fire strong but effective and maintain a steady rhythm... This makes a kind of *poteen*. *Poteen* itself being a corruption of *'uisge potuin'* which means little pot whisky, ie illcit... *'uisge'* is the gaelic for water not whisky, for the real term is *'uisge beatha'* which means *'water of life'*, or *'eau de vie'* or *'aqua vitae'*. Whisky is today taken to mean Scotch Whisky distilled from malted barley grain but the *'water of life'* could be based on anything, even old car tyres, rotten fruit or even rhubarb. The skill is getting something drinkable which will not poison your friends, or make them go blind or rot their livers...

Every so often in the Indian newspapers there are cases of whole villages being wiped out at weddings with someone's specially prepared lethal concoction, a bit like antifreeze in the Austrian wine... or was it the olive oil ?

An improvement to the simple method is however to use a pressure cooker, a length of plastic hose, an empty gallon oil can fitted with a copper coil in which are placed glass beads, and through the can a water jacket of continuous cold water is fed, usually through a hose pipe from the kitchen sink... the heating up is easily done on Rayburns, but a camping gas cooker will do. I am sure it has been done in the Westcountry since time immemorial on various stoves and hobs, though pressure cookers have only been around for about seventy years... no doubt John Cluett's friends used a marvellous contraption, probably the old copper boiler in the corner of the wash house when it wasn't full of dirty washing.

But then in the colonies things have advanced at a brisker pace... In New Zealand it is now perfectly legal to distil your own... so long as it is not commercial. If you blind yourself and suffer from side-effects to your sense and sensibilities through drinking methanol rather than ethanol, that is your own concern. You can poison your neighbours but not the world at large, or to be more precise you can give it away, but not sell it. So *Drinker Beware.* A little knowledge of Chemistry is a very dangerous thing, like the production of home-made fire-works. If you get it wrong, you get it very wrong and it maybe the last thing you maybe ever do...

Even today in parts of the Appalachian mountains you do well to stay away from smoke rising in remote valleys. They shoot first and ask questions later... Hard Cider is made by hard men. On the other side of the coin a Hungarian friend of mine told me that her mother who came out of Hungary in 1956 and has lived in Surbiton ever since, always collected up all the pears and fruit she could, and distilled it on her Rayburn for thirty years just for her husband without realising it was in any way illegal... So Hungarian women pensioners and Blue Grass Kentucky farmers have got something in common, although it is unlikely that shotguns are kept by the front door in Surbiton.

But you never know, the desire to keep one's activities way from prying eyes of neighbours is the same anywhere... No doubt with the memories of Russian tanks on the streets in Budapest, a little pear and plum brandy was very welcome and so it should be...

But these little experiments are only the tip of the iceberg. No doubt the monks in Benedictine & Cistercian monasteries were hard at it in their laboratories, for medicinal purposes of course, cough mixture for the Abbot... and no doubt they were given special dispensation from vespers when the still was going... more going on in the cloisters than meets the eye... and all that flitting backwards and forwards to the continent, boning up on technique. It has long been said that the Dissolution of the Monasteries scattered all sorts of knowledge and without their stills the monks would have been at a loss... the still quiet voice of God... maybe some were taken in by the big houses and given a shed to practice in. Curiously the first use of the word *still* is recorded in 1533 dangerously close to the Dissolution, though other much earlier words such as the Arabic *alembic* or retort are used.

But monasteries may well have been as careful about their activities then as people are today... the tax aspect, the Inland Revenue, Customs and Exercise may have been just as plentiful then as they are today... And what with tithes operating and Rome in the background... Any references to distilling in monastic records would be interesting particularly if the monastery had cider orchards as part of its estate or tribute...

Useful as ever Worlidge comes up trumps and mentions *cider brandy* twice... About young cider he says :

"because of its innocency it yielding also a good spirit which may probably prove a vehicle answerable to that of other wine : at least it may make a very good brandy(which when the fruit is grown more common) in plentiful years may be experimented and improved."

Then again he says :

"for then you may after due fermentation extract spirits, vulgarly called brandy in great plenty, very excellent, quick and burning..."

There is no mention of method or apparatus for distillation, which is unusual as Worlidge is usually forthcoming on all matters in great detail, but no doubt it was still regarded as a secret art and there was no sense in broadcasting the means to undermine a no doubt lucrative under the counter trade.

Another source however from around the same time,

1684, goes into slightly greater detail. This is from *Aphorisms on the new way of Improving Cider* by Richard Haines :

"take eager, very hard or sowre Cider (for that yields by much the more Spirits) twelve gallons; distil it as other Spirits are distill'd, in a Copper Body and Head, and a refrigeratory Worm running through a Cask of Cold Water, under whose Beak a Receiver is placed. From which, with a gentle Fire, draw off two gallons of Cider Brandy, or Spirits, for the use of... "

This is the real thing without a doubt, though the ratios of cider to spirit are higher than one would expect today, but then the ciders may have been up to 10% or more. The usual ratio today with cider @ approx 6.5 % is about 10:1 . So it was certainly worth doing but then again, they were up against first of all, smuggled liquor, mainly French brandy, and then Rum from the West Indies which may have been cheaper in the South West than going to all the lengths and risks of distilling up one's own concoctions. And then of course in the eighteenth century there was the problem of cheap Dutch gin which also took over from cider in the towns as a cheap drink. But that was not till a little later, so graphically depicted by Hogarth who must be one of the few artists to have roundabout and fly over named after him, and that's in Chiswick.

But even so the British attitude to distilling is a difficult one and it may well be that certain Puritan attitudes which had more or less stamped out distilling on religious grounds were later reinvented with Methodism and tee-totalling. Though it would appear that with the Restoration in 1660 that the art of distilling took off again... Certainly by 1710 in the reign of Queen Anne it is clear from Cider statutes and the tax thereon, that cider for distilling was taxed separately, a situation that carried on well into the reign of George III and probably until the new distilling laws came to the fore in the 1823. So there is almost 150 years of cider distilling since Worlidge's time to be taken into account, thus forming a fairly formidable pedigree. No doubt it was regarded as a cheap alternative to brandy from France... the price of *cider brandy* per hogshead would be interesting...

Even the 1930 *OED* refers to the term *cider brandy*... No doubt the vogue for whisky drinking in preference to brandy took over with the establishments of large industrial distilleries north of the border, and the essentially West Country artisan distilling expertise either died a quiet death or, far more likely, simply went underground in various remote farmhouses...

Fortunately in Normandy and Brittany this was not the case, and the industry has grown from strength to strength... suffice it to say that the first active 'Calvados' still to be legally imported here and worked was by Bertie Bulmer in Hereford back in 1984 which still produces a liquor aptly named *King Offa*, who was keen on dykes. But that was strictly for museum educational purposes... you understand... It can be seen to this day alongside the Museum of Cider in Hereford and a very good museum it is too, with acres of archive upstairs. Apparently King Offa had a beautiful daughter called Eadburh who, in a fit of rage, mistakenly poisoned her husband instead of his friend, who had apparently insulted her. She fled in horror to France where the Emperor Charlemagne took pity on her and installed her in a nunnery, but her behaviour so shocked the nuns that she was expelled and finally spent her days, as the last of the Mercian Royal line, begging from pilgrims on the streets of Pavia in Lombardy. St Boniface writing in 747 says that there were a great many English women of bad morals in the city. Even Alfred's sister died there... So problems on the continent for English Royal families are nothing new... the press in the Eighth and Ninth century must have had a field day...

But to return to the story of high spirits closer to home,

the second and much larger distilling venture took place in Somerset a few years later in 1989 and resulted in the Somerset Cider Brandy Company being formed, based on the cider made at Burrow Hill, near the picturesque village of Kingsbury Episcopi, which is somewhere between Langport and Martock. Indeed it is quite hard to find and rightly so, but keep looking for a small hill with a single tree on top of it, and you won't go far wrong. If you can get to the *Rusty Axe* you are within spitting distance...

First they had a small still which can be seen at Brympton d'Evercy near Yeovil. This no longer operates and then they bought several more stills including a beautiful swan-necked still, all polished copper and elegant curves that could be taken everywhere and still is... There was another mobile still which now sits under a walnut tree surrounded by chickens and there were the two operating stills, kept in the neighbouring village of Thorney, but this, only after formidable piles of paperwork, endless visits and inspections, iron bars, alarm systems and Alcatraz-type security. The first one to be installed and to have her paperwork and joints approved was called *Josephine* and she was resurrected in the back of an old milk factory which in its turn had been used for storing ammunition during the war, so it was strong and vandal-proof, at least by Somerset standards.

Josephine is quite a sight with pipes flowing everywhere, portly and with a bit of middle age spread she sits perched on her plinth awaiting customs. Matronly and with some style she raises steam or rather alcohol and once fired up gives of her best, quantity and quality in her case to some extent going hand in hand. But to rely on one still was too dodgy and anyway it was felt that *Josephine* might be feeling lonely and sad and pining for her home country, so the company in its wisdom made another trip to Normandy and imported *Fifi* on the back of yet another lorry. She was small fast and pretty, like the current *au pair* after whom she was named. *Fifi* was younger but gave her spirit faster but with great character. Any interest in *Calvados* or *cider brandy* they figured was an advantage. She joined after a couple of years and so it was that brace of working *Calvados* stills took root in Somerset close to the banks of the River Parrett. The whole operation only about six feet above the flood levels. But in Somerset six feet is a long way, it's a fathom...

The French experts in Normandy gave the company every encouragement and were only too willing to part with the old stills. *Josephine* and *Fifi* were both built in Paris, *'Fabrique en Paris'* before the war so they survived the *'Occupation'* intact... and have been lovingly tinkered with ever since... indeed when they were being set up, long phone calls through interpreters were conducted from Somerset to Normandy, with old men who still serviced various stills, the skill, like that of the distiller, passing from father to son. Indeed it is a curious trait in Normandy that the men who make the cider cannot own the orchards, which allows free market forces to work. It keeps the price of cider apples buoyant... whereas here it has stagnated at around £90 a ton for the last 20 years... and farmers got bound into long-term contracts with cider works which did not always work to their advantage in a bumper year, when the works would turn their apples away...

As a distiller you have to have a licence and this is very difficult to obtain, you have to have the distillery more than two miles away from your cider farm, it has to be clearly observed from a public road so that the law can keep an eye on you...

In fact it has to fulfil all the obligations as if you were wearing a kilt and were North of the border... Scottish Whisky Distillery regulations are formidable and designed so that no Scotsman even from Glasgow can circumvent them, though no doubt they have been contravened, on numerous occasions in the past... This means about 68 different locks and lead seals stamped and inspected regularly by a Customs and Excise officer, samples of cider taken, samples of spirit taken, samples of *low wines* and *feints* which are recycled, volumes measured meticulously, the alcohol content measured to the nearest ten decimal points and the revenue worked out. This particular distillery which is small by Scottish standards but about the same size as a high quality malt distillery, gets through about £10,000 of revenue a day when it is operational, but the tax is not extracted till the spirit comes out of bond, i.e. when it has aged and is fit for bottling... and of course drinking...

When you arrive for a day's distilling you get up early in the morning and arrive for work in the dark at about 6 am. It is usually February and cold or flooded. Your first task is to unlock the various locks and fiendish devices, which enable you to work the stills... fill in the log which has to be kept every minute of the day, signed and countersigned... like the ship's log, and not lost overboard, a grubby chart plotting the longitude and latitude, of each day's progress, circumnavigating the oceans of cider that arrive every day, in glistening stainless steel containers towed by tractors and mounted on old farm trailers, pumped aboard, and the cycle started again.

The second task is to light the main boilers and this is gas fired, and this is usually the worst part, for you have to wield lighted newspapers, rush and turn the gas on, lie down low and reach in with your arm under the still. This is a hazardous operation which can take your eyebrows off, but once ignition is achieved, and the main part is filled with cider, it takes about 45 minutes to reach the temperature required for distillation... Indeed the whole operation heaves and grunts a little to itself till the heat runs through the copper pipes and the heady atmosphere soon regenerates itself within the building and resembles that of the engine room of a tramp steamer in the tropics... warm, humid and with an air of expectation.

Above the boiling vat is a wonderful column called the fractionating column, which has five or six layers and on the inside they have what look like small mushrooms made out of copper, which allow the vapour to come up from below, condense a bit, then go on up to the next layer, where the same thing happens. This ensures that only the best goes on over This is the important part, where the various fractions are separated, and only the one you want, hopefully, gets carried over into the condensing column. And here is the clever bit, the cold cider coming in is used to cool the vapour as it condenses, and the cold cider in its turn is pre-warmed before it enters the pot, a neat arrangement which saves on fuel and costs, the technical term being, I suppose, a heat exchanger...

This is a continuous still which can be worked non stop if need be, and a sixteen hour shift is not unheard of, being split into two eight hour shifts. Many of the earlier stills were pot stills which required heating up one pot and letting it cool. This is good for small quantities but tedious if you want a regular supply. One story I heard from Brittany via Gloucestershire, was that the condensing column was kept on an old farm cart, and once the heating process was judged to be over, the condensing vessel was separated and the cart driven at full speed by horse into a ford or a pond to cool it, amidst much merriment, steam, ducks , and no doubt creaking of joints. The idea being to help condense the *Calvados* quickly. Primitive but no doubt effective.

But in Somerset it is an almost clinical operation with *low wines* going back into the vat, the temperatures of both stills juggled, the hydrometers read every half an hour, everything monitored, even the sandwiches and the weather...

In France every family member is, I heard allowed five litres of *Calvados* at every night's distilling, before tax is paid but it must be done at night... and so at every farm, a farmer will get as many relations together as possible, aunts, mothers-in-law, cousins six times removed, all are wheeled out, and they have to stay the whole evening, heads are counted, and in a village where everyone is related, the whole village more or less turns out night after night at separate farms. Most of these stills are mobile and can be taken from farm to farm... Distilling can be done outdoors and often is, but the penalties in dealing in illegal *hooch* are severe, the fine being I believe about £1000. but everybody takes a healthy attitude to it. It's just in England that its been so long since small-scale distilling was allowed that its regarded almost as Devil's work, and handled very carefully. No doubt the horrors of cheap Dutch gin, so accurately depicted by Hogarth, still float around the corridors of Whitehall.

Some think the colonies are backward, but far from it, they often take the lead. Indeed brewing your own beer was illegal I believe till the sixties, such a tight hold here did the breweries have on the nation and their leisure hours. But then it is only in the last hundred years, farm workers have had the vote. Women had to wait till after the First World War and then they had to be 30 or over. But in New Zealand, women had the vote a good thirty years before they did here, in 1893. Who knows in the next century what legislation might be lurking. Pigs may fly ...

But to return to the still... To run one is a tricky business, you have to get it balanced and the liquor coming off at 70 per cent i.e. nearly twice as strong as you would normally drink it,then it will run regular as clockwork. You can get it stronger, but the quantity drops. There is always an optimum temperature and this is best helped by getting the distance between the two columns just right so that the temperature-drop across the divide is just enough to encourage the vapour to start condensing.

The stills only had one temperature gauge each and that on the return pipe from the condensing column. Then there was the hydrometer reading to be taken behind three sets of glass, bobbing up and down in the distillate. At this point you could take a sample but only a very small one. The one sure way of knowing whether the whole apparatus was working correctly, was simply to reach up with your hand on the condensing column and to feel the temperature at a certain rivet. If you could just put your hand there comfortably without it getting burnt, it was at optimum temperature, and everything went smoothly. Your only control is the inlet valve for raw cider and the outlet valve for the spirit, which of course was clear.

As it got hot in the distillery it was essential to keep the doors ajar, to stop yourself nodding off, or letting the fumes get the better of you, but if the doors were open too far the slightest wind would set things awry... even somebody walking into the room would alter the temperature slightly. Every time 25 litres of spirit was collected in an old dairy milk jar, you pressed a button and the spirit would be pumped to a large vat, which would be measured at the beginning and end of the day, and then when full would be decanted into the barrels in the bond, which was an art in itself.

Any leakage or spillage of barrels bursting would be accountable, although there is always what is known as the *Angels' Share*, the amount allowed for natural evaporation or take up in the barrel, and each barrel behaves slightly differently. Some are young and dry, others are old and black. Each has to be inspected before it is filled, and then carefully weighed and measured. The atmosphere in the bond is similar to that of a great cellar and it needs cool damp air at about 10°C. To see hundreds of barrels all filled with cider brandy petering off into the distance is a great sight... from blossom to bottle a minimum of five years and then the process of testing each barrel for colour, smell, taste, oak , Sherry. Bourbon, White Rum... all blended, then brought down by easy stages to 42% the palate tickled, nurtured, tested.

The art, the knack, like navigating through a maze of islands to find the lost continent, the Holy Grail, a manual of distilling rediscovered, the alternative communion, the right spirit, strong smooth and blended, robust full and round, rebellious in body when young like teenagers, but laced with character when mature. The ten years nearly up and ready for the Millennium.

1990 was a massive cider crop and a massive distilling year next spring. Nature getting itself all organised... That year also brought great floods and the next village of Muchelney was cut off for two weeks. I used to get up on the distillery roof by way of a ladder and survey the flood waters in every direction... almost an island again...

And then there is '*Eau de Vie*'. fiery but good and very appley and excellent on strawberries or in fruit salad, or with coffee as you would with *grappa or calvados* in a French sheep or cattle market, to improve the bidding. Then there is *apple aperitif*, known in the past as *Royal Cider, cider brandy* cut back with single variety apple juice and taken down to the strength between sherry and port. Very popular with those who don't want the full on effect of brandy in the middle of the day... an appetiser, neither too sweet nor too dry, well rounded and very drinkable...

But that's enough of distilling. Age does wonders, but the original spirit has to have the character there, otherwise the journey, the vision, the *mystique* is lacking... *Cider brandy* no doubt has a long life and the history that goes with it is an essential part of the rural economy. John Worlidge would I hope be pleased by today's efforts and be of good opinion as to the quality of the product. Three hundred years are, after all, in the history of the apple, only a twinkling. Who knows in another hundred years the South West could be as productive as the Glens of Scotland or the *Pays d'Auge*.

The great danger is being bought out and closed down or run as a 'lost' leader. The *Spirit of Somerset* is I think one to be reckoned with, and the very first bottle of ten-year old, smooth, rounded, powerful as an ox but subtle as stream, with more than just a *'hint of orchard on the tongue'*. Here there is a true explosion of fragrance and colour that lifts not just the palate but the whole rolling landscape of an ancient tradition. No wonder the monks kept it to themselves... and this new enterprise in Somerset is only just beginning...

Cider does relax the belly... aid concoction, depress Vapours resist Melancholy, Spleen, Pleurisy, Strangury, and being sweetened with sugar abate inveterate Colds...

Capt Sylas Taylor in Evelyn's *Pomona*   1664

The bacon one can only dream about, but the excellent cider, like a golden '*vin de pays*', solaces the historical traveller....

WG Hoskins 1954

Part Nine

Last Rites - Getting Back from Work

At the end of the day when the last cheese has been put up and the boards are stacked, the cheese cloths are hung up on odd nails like monk's habits, cloths that have been folded twenty or thirty times during the day. Cloths that will, if left heaped, heat up with the fermentation process and get stale and musty, so the air must get to them overnight. Also a cheese that has been pressed out will over-heat, in the same way that hay can combust on its own if too green. The cloths are periodically washed in an industrial cleaner and then finished off in the work's washing machine to get the bits of fine apple out. The last cheese is left in the press wet, and will be pressed out first thing the next morning, so the rhythm isn't broken. With two presses the system is very efficient indeed. A very nineteenth century way to work, and not too much 'down' time. Chairs even at tea breaks are a rare and much sought after commodity. The work-force can't be having too much of a good time otherwise you wouldn't have that marvellous 'after work' feeling...

The pit is emptied, not just of apples periodically to clean the slats out, but to get the dirty water out that circulates all day bobbing the apples along. It is amazing what gets into a load of apples. The old Belfast sink, or dirt trap, gets shovelled out for the last time. One bit of grit or metal or cartridge case in the mill is serious business, as the blades go round very fast and when blunt can cause back-log problems with apples piling up and over-spilling from the hopper upstairs... All these things are seen to, and watched-out for during the day, as well as the various water levels, pressure gauges and machinery noise.

The mill is cleaned out and hosed down, careful not to wet the electrics. Old pomace is gathered up from various crevices and the whole cider house is cleaned down. Odd piles of leaves and half scrunched apples are put into the muck spreader and will be spread down the moor in the morning.

Usually it takes about half an hour to clear up. At the same time, the last cheese is going up, the belts going round and round, the valves and pressure gauges are checked and odd bearings greased. The machinery is old but it work's wonderfully well. The boards are washed down and at the end of every week pressure-washed and then stacked in herring bone patterns to dry out as they would heat up as well. Boards that are constantly checked for flaws and replaced with new or repaired ones. They take enormous pressure and distribute it throughout the cheese.

For several years my job at the end of the day was down the bottom of the pit under the wooden sides getting the last of the water and dirt out, not a pleasant job, during the last few years I have had the 'upper crust' bits to clean, where the mill is situated, and you have to crawl around on your hands and knees picking up stray apples and pomace. At times you can really feel the vibration when the presses are going up but the beams are wooden and have a fair bit of 'give' in them. Through cracks in the floor boards you can peer down to the cider house below.

Usually at the tail-end of the season it is dark by the end of the day, so we normally try to go up the hill in the lunch hour, give the dog a quick run chasing rabbits and see what's about... There is a single sycamore tree, with a swing off one branch, as well as horses, sheep, a triangulation point and an extraordinary view in all directions.

To the south lies Ham Hill, the largest Iron Age fort in Europe... it dominates the skyline as indeed the *Durotriges* tribe did in the centuries before the Roman invasion. They monitored a trade route which stretched to the south coast and France in one direction and down the River Parrett to Wales and Ireland in the other. Burrow Hill must have been an important lookout point for anyone coming up the river or across the then marshes... who knows if they made cider. There is still a fair bit of mistletoe in the trees which can occur naturally with birds or deliberately be slipped in under the bark where it takes root. Eventually it will kill the tree but not for a fair while.

To the north is the town of Langport, the cider monument at Curry Rivel, the church towers of Muchelney and Huish, and there in the distance Glastonbury Tor with its ruined tower, Avalon, hippies, crystals and of course the famous festival... At one time Michael Eavis had me doing wind powered sheep-shearing which was an interesting diversion, but it's the cider and the big blue double-decker cider bus which often makes as much impact as the music on people at the festival, being as it is first stop off the main stage, and people having as they do, a terrible thirst for the apple what with all that dust... and strange substances... A fair proportion of the cider made every year gets sold at Glastonbury and other festivals... if the people don't come to you take it to the people... From Burrow Hill you also get a good view of Mendip and the main television mast... Mendip that keeps Bristol at bay, what with Wookey and Cheddar and various swallets... the deep holes that can suddenly open up and swallow cows, streams and even landrovers.

In contrast to the limestone quarries in the distance, the Somerset Levels abound in peat, withies and wildfowl. It is a tranquil and productive landscape which is tended more like a garden than farm land, for these are small farmers and the land still means a lot to them, and their survival depends very much on their diverse skills of husbandry.

After work is finished, the cider workers can if they wish, gather in the cider house proper. The doors are closed and then glasses brought out, to test to mull things over, talk to the dog, get in a gallon for the evening...

In the early days of the distilling business, much debate was carried out and the main part of the sampling done here. At Christmas time mulled cider is on tap from a big tea urn and this keeps the pneumonia and bronchitis away, as it can get pretty damp working there all the time. The other items we take to stem the damp, are small but highly effective menthol lozenges called '*Fisherman's Friends*' which come from *Lofthouse's* in Fleetwood and we refer to them as *cyanide tablets*... just in case the going gets a bit rough with all that repetitive and tiring work... it takes it out of you, no mistake making over 20 cheeses a day, trundling them around the cider house and then unloading them. That's fifteen tons loaded and eight tons off loaded near enough. I try to issue *cyanide tablets* at certain times of day and they do work marvellously well. Judging by the amount we get through we should get a free batch of them down in Somerset from the makers every now and then, though the cider does taste a bit peculiar after taking one... all that menthol, liquorice and eucalyptus oil.

Ironically apple pips have some cyanide in them and they taste like almonds, but you would have to eat a very large number before you became ill. As an aside, I am reliably informed, that it is the prisons not the remote farmsteads that represent the hot-bed of illicit distilling. And before the modern drug era, *hooch* in prisons was very much a currency, evading Revenue under the Government's very nose... But Revenue is a touchy subject in Somerset after Lord Bute and the so called *'Scottish Yolk'* of 1763. Independence at all costs. Why only in 1982, the local farmers, enraged at the Government telling them how to farm on West Sedgemoor, burnt images of Conservationists and the Agriculture Minister in the carpark of the Black Smock... a pub alongside the River Parrett where a fair bit of cider is still drunk... needless to say they got more money and the mock lynchings did the trick.

After work is over and you have had a small glass of cider, you hang up the smock, walk through the darkened yard, back past the vast piles of apples. A day's work doesn't look much, because any space you may have made in the yard, will almost certainly have been filled by other trailer loads. The only measure you have is by looking up at the vast vat and working how many feet it has filled in the day...

You walk through the tail end of the yard into the top of the orchard, go to the back of the van and change your boots for shoes, which are more comfortable to drive in... All day standing up in wellies on wet concrete can be a bit much, and tea breaks are a little short and there is a lack of chairs already alluded to, and so at the end of the day to put it bluntly, you are completely knackered...

You start the van, much to the pleasure of the dog, who is by now getting rather tired of office work. And then it is out of the farm by a potholed track, through the top end of the bush orchard, passing palette loads of new bottles, old trailers, fork lifts, bits of tractor and the caravans of the apple pickers, as well as piles of black wrapped big bale silage. I head off down the track, turn right onto the road to Kingsbury... Small cottages abound. Some painted with bright yellow or green fences. Corrugated iron is painted red, here are a few basket makers and sheds full of withies. There is a turning to Lower Burrow which is well tucked away, that's where some of the pomace ends up...

Eventually you arrive at the *Rusty Axe* which has a large axe nailed up outside on the name board, for those that can't

read, and then carry on down into Kingsbury itself. Odd orchards appear on the right and left, in various differing conditions.

Kingsbury has some large thatched houses and others made of red brick which have spectacular verandahs... there was wealth here at one time no doubt... You pass the *Wyndham Arms*, named after the family that owned much of the land until the 1950's. On the right is the village shop and Post Office and there opposite the Methodist church the village lock-up, a small but well built octagonal cell made from hamstone such as an early Irish hermit would have been proud of. Discreet and self contained, in a prime position, ample parking and a strong front door... It is in here that they would place any drunks, cattle thieves or people causing a more than usual nuisance of themselves, like pickled apple pickers and cider makers. Lock-ups are rare in Somerset, only about eight survive but they no doubt served their purpose and could be easily be brought back into use again today... A night in the cooler would dampen a few of the local spirits now given to throwing stones at windows in neighbouring towns and be a lot cheaper and save on all that police paper work... Maybe they have been drinking too much *white cider*...all that glucose gone to the head...

Then you pass on down the road towards Thorney... Occasionally the odd *'drove'* branches off to the left and goes on down towards the moor. On the right behind the hedge and one field in, is the river... At Thorney there is an old mill which still has the machinery in it, and the wheel which is slightly the worse for wear but still goes round, built 1866. Here there is also a weir and the remains of a lock gate. A mill pool frequented by eels and large carp... Thorney used to have a coal depot here and the coal came up the river by barge from Wales via Bridgwater... One field is still called *'coal heaps'* and lumps of coal occasionally still appear in the bank. Apparently in the old days, apples, usually *Morgan*

Sweets would be sent back to Wales for the miner's lunch box, which was taken with *Caerphilly* Cheese. And maybe there was a great call for cider in the valleys, as it did quench the thirst more successfully and was cheaper. Even in Yorkshire and the North East, cider was regarded as a working man's drink, being twice the strength of beer, you only had to drink half as much...

These days we have no real concept either of hard manual work in very hot conditions or indeed any idea of what it must have been like to get the first fruit of the season, so cosseted are we with '*jet-setting*' apples and other fruit we barely know the names of. The taste of commercial success is, it seems, is to have no taste at all. We rave on about *organic* produce, surely all produce is *organic* unless it is tampered with in some way, and so maybe everything that is **not** *organic* should have a sticker... and in the same way that you see *Country of origin*, or worse still *Produce of more than one country*, we should perhaps have stickers that say **County of origin**, then we could identify with various regions in Britain and build up a working knowledge of our own countryside once again... in other words *Landscape produce* again.

Indeed in the 13th Cent on a regional level the links with Wales and Somerset were much stronger in the past as it was only just across the water, and still is... In the old days you had to go across the River Severn at Gloucester which meant that Cardiff was about as far away as London, at least by road. Indeed the good citizens of Bridgwater were caught loading vessels with cattle and supplies for Owen Glendower during the uprisings...

But to return to Thorney there was a withy factory here,. and a milk factory as well as a halt on the railway line. Now there is a haulage firm and the *Somerset Cider Brandy Company* which lives in the back of the red brick building, with its own bonded warehouse. Then there is the house of the eel smoker who specialises in producing some of the

very best of smoked items in the South West... the smoked cheddar is out of this world.

From Thorney then, which was once an island, you pass to Muchelney which was also an island *In Time of Flood*, and still is... Here is the potter John Leach, grandson of Bernard. Indeed outside his front door was the last piece of dry land for several miles in Feb 1990 and people would row up to get supplies. School children went to school on a tractor and trailer sitting on a line of straw bales... John Leach whose pots are much admired and collected. He is, like them, full, round and robust. Earlier on this year, 1999, he made a three handled Wassail mug which holds three pints and takes some beating. The old mugs, where you could hand it to the next in line, hopefully without spilling a drop. Beyond lies the main village and then there is Muchelney Abbey itself, small enough to be left relatively undemolished. The Abbot's house was used as a farmhouse until the beginning of this century and the Priest's house opposite, dating from the fourteenth century, which was on the point of collapse before it was restored... It may well be that the Muchelney Monks, who were always being admonished for their bad behaviour, appropriation of church funds, loose living, prolonged absence and avoidance of prayers and obligatory ritual, did do some distilling on the side. Indeed if they did not, it would be very surprising... the wealth of the Abbot's parlour is plain for all to see... an ideal spot in winter all cut off and with a large tithe barn to experiment in... there were even rumours of monks having their own bedrooms and of women not only entering the monks private quarters but staying longer than they should perhaps have done, if the monastic vow was to be taken at all seriously... but then this was Somerset, and the Abbey cut off in winter by flood water, a lonely place, and the need to keep warm no doubt inviting creature comfort...

Smoked eels and cider brandy no doubt appeared on their copious menus... copper pipe would be an interesting little addition to their shopping lists, as would retorts or glass apparatus... One local character says that where the Abbey is, there used to be a '*damn good orchard* ' until they put all them stones there and called it an *Ancient Monument*.

From Muchelney you pass along a new causeway towards Langport. It is this road which floods most commonly in winter as there is not only the junction of the River Parrett and the Yeo but also, a little further up, at Midelney, the junction of the Parrett and the Isle. The banks cannot take all the water so it is allowed to overflow naturally. Here flooding is a *fact of nature* and a *fact of life*, and often I have had to drive to and from work through floods. Sometimes in orchards you see the whole apple crop bobbing up and down in the slight swell.

Once in Huish you pass the slaughter-house on your right and then by the church you can go left through the East gate into Langport down the hill towards the *Langport Arms*, or turn the other way towards *Eli's* an old pub which still has an original tap room, and no bar. It has been in the same family for over a hundred years and always passed down through the women folk, who maybe better at keeping it in profit, rather than the profit getting the better of you...

If you keep on going past the school you get to *old Kelways*, the nursery which was famous over a hundred years ago and specialises in Irises and Peonies and had I believe some of the earliest commercially heated greenhouses. The wonderful old buildings have now been restored and turned into a restaurant and Council offices. Before that it had been abandoned for several years and you could find old catalogues and despatch tickets in the outhouses. Then you go along past the *new Kelways* which still flourishes and then hit a fairly fast bit of road which dips down and then up the other side.

At the bottom lies *Wagg Drove*. This is supposedly the site of the Battle of Langport in 1645 where the Royalist forces,

although occupying the higher ground on the Langport side, were eventually dislodged by a daring uphill cavalry charge. It was the last real battle in the South West during the Civil War and the Royalists fled to Bridgwater but not before they had 'fired' Bow Street. The castle in Bridgwater was supposed to be impregnable and the Royalists thought themselves safe. Lady Christabella Wyndham is said to have distinguished herself when Cromwell and Fairfax formally asked for the surrender before laying siege proper. As she had been wet nurse to the future Charles II, and was proud of her assets and Royal connections, she bared her breast on the ramparts and is said to have shouted out, "*This breast has suckled a Royal child... Up Yours*"or words to that effect, and then as a true Somerset Royal, taken a pot shot at Cromwell, missed him but killed an ADC who just happened to be alongside. So incensed was Cromwell at the affront to his modesty that he ordered the cannon balls to be pre-heated so that when they sailed over the walls, the town caught fire, which is why there isn't much left of Old Bridgwater. Others say that the Royalists 'fired' the rest to leave it smouldering after they fled. Of Lady Christabella it is said that she escaped to the low countries and seduced her former charge on his sixteenth birthday. Certainly the Wyndhams were an interesting family and on certain occasions the women showed more mettle than the men. It would be marvellous to have her story confirmed... Interestingly enough Bridgwater is home to several interesting apple varieties : *Bridgwater Pippin, Glory of the West, Golden Knob*. Perhaps they should have had a *Lady Christabella* or a *Monmouth Rebel,* but there is still time. Names with a personal history are so much better than long numbers with pre-fixes that sound more like motorway systems... M27, A1, M62 etc.

But to return to the road you pass the *Halfway House* at the top which specialises in Real Ale and has won awards for various things... Then you enter Somerton with its assortment of old coaching pubs. Once reputedly the capital of Wessex, though this may have just been a stopping off place for a Saxon king on the move, who may or may not have had an *Apple Coronation*. But there is a fine square built in blue lias. It was here that a few rebels were hung after the Battle of Sedgemoor, as they were in every town as an example to deter future uprisings. As it was, it was the last real battle on English soil, but even before I moved into the area, I had an electrician who wired my old house in Shaftesbury who said that his ancestor had been hung drawn and quartered here in the square in Somerton... And it was not just that, the bodies, once quartered, were then boiled in a mixture of oil, salt and pitch to preserve them and then displayed in choice public locations for up to two years. Better than video nasties...

Even now Judge Jeffreys is not the most popular of people in Somerset and one wonders how much cider had to do with people joining up to the rebel cause. For many it would seem they had nothing much to lose, and for those that were deported a new life beckoned in the West Indies as hard labour on plantations. Even to this day in Barbados, certain Somerset dialect words still exist. And although they were intended to stay for ten years, they were pardoned at the five year stage after James II had fled in a barge down the Thames, or was it a rowing boat ? much to the annoyance of the plantation owners who had bought the rebels for ten years work. They naturally enough felt cheated... it was after all a business deal... Some returned, others went to America by the back door so to speak, no doubt with a healthy non conformity, an independent streak and a slight rebelliousness.

But at the end of a long hard day, there is little thought of rebellion... only a hot bath. This is the way home and when you are tired and wet through, the prospect of a warm fire, hot soup and a good meal washed down with mulled cider is by far the best part of the day.

So even in one day's work the whole history of Cider comes to bear, it is still moving on, developing, evolving. A long and interesting tradition which has a major stake in parts of our landscape and even our notions of paradise, whether it be walled gardens or acres of blossom stretching as far as the eye can see. Apples have, at their heart, something very special which appeals to the human race, and the real apples of this country are an endangered species as perhaps are the finest of the farmhouse cider makers.

As always apples take you back to your childhood, and those memories lurk, in the back of your mind, for the rest of your life. Family associations are also very important and so I will leave some of the last words on a very practical note to a good friend, the writer John Fowles who lives in West Dorset. He is partial to good cider... especially the *aperitif*.

John's extract comes from *'The Tree'* and is a poignant reminder of the role of fruit in communicating something special and even delicate between fathers and sons. Indeed orchards by their very nature have a tendency to involve the whole family. This extract comes from his own childhood and the soils not of the Westcountry but of the then, new Essex suburbs. John's father was a London tobacconist and obviously like many who had been through the First World War and the horrors of it, chose, quite wisely, to concentrate on fruit growing in his spare time.

" *My father's trees, already happy in the alluvial clay of the area, must have been among the most closely pruned, cosseted and prayed for in the whole of England, and regularly won him prizes at local shows. They were certainly the finest, flavoured of their varieties-many increasingly rare, these supermarket days, because of their commercial disadvantages, such as tender flesh or the mysterious need to be 'eaten from the tree'-that I have ever tasted. Memories of them, of their names and flavours,* **Charles Ross** *and* **Lady Sudely**, **Peasgood's Nonsuch** *and* **King of the Pippins**, *haunt me still. Even the more popular kinds he grew,* *such as the Comice, or the Mozart and Beethoven of English pomology,* **James Grieve** *and* **Cox's Orange**, *acquired on his cunningly stunted trees a richness and subtlety I have rarely met since. This may have been partly because he knew exactly when they should be eaten. A* **Comice** *pear may take many weeks to ripen in store, but it is at its peak for only a day. Perfection in the* **Grieve** *is almost as transient."*

Indeed my own grandfather who had also survived four years in the trenches turned to fruit and fruit growing in his spare time, and I will never forget the smell of his apple store in the autumn and the way he laid each apple out on wooden trays and monitored the temperature, the air flow, the different species and the odd invasions of mice... Even now in Somerset, my own father carries on the tradition in his own way by perfecting his jam making techniques, and so takes on the old ladies of the village at their own game. Twice a year he enters his jam for the village show and the competition results are religiously pinned up on the back of his kitchen door...

But the plight of the orchards and the place of the fine eating apple is very much in the balance. To get some idea of how much we have lost, you have to go back to the year 1883, the year before the farm workers were given the vote, and visit the Great Vinery of Chiswick Gardens where the National Apple Congress was in full swing. It was early October and there were over 10,000 separate dishes of apples, grouped by counties from all over the country each with four apples on each dish. That is over 40,000 apples in peak condition, representing over 1,500 varieties. The smell must have been extraordinary, fragrant, powerful and exciting... the biggest collection of different apples ever gathered in the world under one roof.

Now we are down to a few varieties that store easily and can be kept at low temperatures indefinitely. One organisation that at least has tried to correct this state of affairs is *Common Ground* who have done so much to raise people's awareness about the plight of fields, hedgerows and orchards and to this end instigated Apple Day in 1990 which has now grown from strength to strength... into a series of national events.

They are not an organisation that you can belong to like the National Trust or the RSPB, but they show people how to start projects like Parish Maps and the importance of recording the local distinctiveness of an area, features such as trees, field names and even rivers, small brooks, wells, and springs. Their main role is to make us all more aware of what we have lost, and what we still have around us. Most of it is still there it is simply that we do not have time to look out for it. But orchards can be cut down in a twinkling and here is an extract from one of their essays.

"When you lose an orchard, you sacrifice not simply a few old trees (bad enough some would say) but you might lose forever varieties particular to that locality, the wild life, the songs, the recipes, the cider/perry/cherry brandy, the hard but social work, the festive gatherings, the look of the landscape, the wisdom gathered over generations about pruning and grafting, about aspect and slope, soil and season, variety and use. In short the cultural landscape is diminished by many dimensions at one blow".

Angela King and Sue Clifford
The Apple, the Orchard, the Cultural Landscape
A Common Ground Essay Sept 1993

Perhaps enough has been said about orchards and apples and cider, but I thought the last word should come from the other side of Dartmoor, the area in which I was brought up, where West Devon borders onto Cornwall. Here the steep sides of the Tamar valley make fruit-growing an ideal occupation, and it was here that I did my first Harvest work and then Turkey-plucking at Christmas time. Cider was always on hand and this seemed perfectly natural for long hard monotonous jobs, and so it was I got to know the cider farm run by Horace Lancaster at a place aptly enough called Felldownhead, just the other side of Milton Abbot. Even to this day I can still recall seeing Horace coming out of his darkened barns rubbing his hands together and cheerfully muttering to himself that:

Bread is the Staff of Life
But Cider is Life itself

A drop or two of cider will do us no harm
No harm .... No harm ....
A drop or two of cider will do us no harm...

Extracts from the Traditional *Wassail* song
collected in Drayton by Cecil Sharp 1903

APPLE HAIKU

Acres of blossom -
Row upon row of neat petals
Pulling them in.

                Orchards of peace,
                Identify the first bite -
                Sweet taste of another world.

Juice flowing between narrow slats -
An orange waterfall
That must be tasted.

                Dark surrounds the vast barrels
                Like a secret veil -
                Months of doing its own thing.

Worth waiting for -
First glass, first sip
The squeak of a tap.

                Stamped into the new cider's passport -
                Silent nod,
                Quiet murmur of approval.

THE SECRET ORCHARD MEETING PLACE

Daughter of blossom, the apple
A saucey little item, sits neatly in your palm,
Exquisite in its pert roundness,
Asking to be admired and handled...

Look for instance, at the much fogotten stalk
The secret timing of its fall from grace,
That has within it's grasp,
The gravity of the situation.

Or else the '*Apple of your Eye*' cradled in the sun,
And plucked in perfection from the tree of life,
The rosie skin that takes a shine,
Protects the inner flesh, firm, crisp and even...

Till young mouths are brought into play,
And teeth sunk into sweet sharpness,
The hint of summer lost in autumn,
Each subtle fragrance stored within the mind,

A host of memories, the DNA of myth, the pips,
Eve's gift, a timely signal, carried down the ages,
Small sanctuary, the source of secret divination,
Sliced through, yields an inner core,

That once discarded, rises up again,
The shadey orchard meeting place for slender youth.
Beneath *The Golden Bough,*
Two song birds within a garden walled.

CIDERMAKING - THE FORGOTTEN MIRACLE

The cider apple is a noble beast,
Not least its rounded shape and form.
Red on white and dressed in green,
Daughter of the crab, pert and sharp.

A bitter little number brought to heel,
And mounded up in countless yards,
Squeezed tightly, acres' promise pressed,
Between hefty thighs of oak and elm.

Ripe juice, a mad cascade run off,
And pumped to monstrous vats,
Where potent yeast works unruly magic,
And heady froth ferments in darkened barns.

Weeks and months pass, as days get longer
Each barrel sampled, tapped into,
Deep reservoirs of superstition
Ancient orchards, gnarled citizens revived,

Communion with the Apple God
And passed from hand to hand,
The clear drop that quenches working thirst.
Rebellious, yet subtle and triumphant,

Vivacious and sparkling,
Filled to the brim and sprightly,
A slender glass of liquid gold
That shimmers in the evening light.

BURROW HILL CIDER FARM

There in the barn dark
Inch by inch
The steady inquisition
The confession extracted
As the press pushes home
Flows ever more freely
Ruddy brown and golden
A river in flood
Whole orchards
The never ending tide
Ebbing and flowing
Mounds of apples
Like long barrows
Lagoons of red and yellow...
Dabinett, Porter's Perfection
Bloody Turk, Yarlington Mill
Tremlett's Bitter, Tom Putt
Their ransomed juice
Vast in their yeast brooding
Broad in the beam
Their froth fermenting bellies
Straps of iron, barrels
A Norman trick
Distilled and fiery

layer by layer
gallon by gallon
begins
bit by bit
life blood of the heathen apple
the stout cheese dripping
like honey
a hive of fruit
pulped and crushed
trailers
acres deep and rounded
tipped and spewed forth
the farm yard filled to bursting
Brown Snout and Chisel Jersey
Stoke Red and Kingston Black
Lambrook Pippin
Royal Somerset
pumped to distant vats
potent and powerful
fecund and fattening
bound with oak
giant and gargantuan...
this drink from apples
hint of orchard on the tongue...

CIDER HAIKU

The orchard fits snuggly
Round our shoulders -
Like an old overcoat.

Caught between slats of ash -
Each cheese
A mountain of apple.

Volume here is all that matters
Taken in at a glance -
Oak that has to tamed.

Invisibly we merge
With the barrels -
Are sucked into their darkness.

All at once we are enveloped
By the brooding silence -
Ten thousand gallons.

Our lives are measured out
In tractors and trailers -
Each load a fraction of an acre.

Hard pressed, the stream of juice
Runs madly from the cheese -
Autumn careering out of control.

Echoing in empty chambers -
The filled,
And the yet to be filled.

Their roundness catapults us
Beyond the common place -
A world apart.

THE SPIRIT LEVEL

The Somerset Cider Brandy Distillery

Josephine and Fifi	shipped in from Normandy
Side by side	circus of shining pipes
Vie with one another	sleek jungle
A brace of calvados stills	copper pipes tangled
Tramp steamers	like an engine room in the tropics
Showing their age a little	resurrected, 'Fabrique en Paris'
Like the au pair...	faithfully fermented
Distilled. condensed	the ship's log, a grubby chart
The longitude and latitude	navigating oceans of cider
Plotted, the orchard's wake	each rivet, each drop
Precious liquid	clocked and tamed
A symphony	hidden behind glass
The copper serpent	a cauldron refined
Hot heady and powerful	yields up its nectar
Clear, aromatic	ardent and sensuous
Level spirit, eau de vie	avant garde mystique.

THE SPIRIT BOND

The Warehouse

Quiet
reformatory,
biding time, twiddling thumbs
in the cool, damp. even darker dark.
Cooper's craft, committed, sectioned, curved
caulked and tapped. A gallery of gargantuan
barrels,hogsheads stacked high,five score fuming
and fiery. Nurtured from blossom to bottle,
Dragon's bite held within oak like gunpowder
kegs about to explode.The Alternative
Communion, hours of reflection, seeking the right
nose. Strong, smooth and blended. robust, full,
round and rebellious in body like teenagers
growing up, sleek as an otter, the spirit's path, an
inner glow, the Angel's share, the knowing
look. A somerset trick, surreptitously
smuggled down the ages
a butt laid
down.

WASSAIL WASSAIL

GOOD 'EALTH TO FARMER AND FARMER'S WIFE
TO ORCHARDS AND THE BEES
AND FARMER'S WORKERS
ON THEIR KNEES
A-PICKIN UP THE APPLES.

GOOD 'EALTH TO FARMER'S DAUGHTER
WE SPIED HER THRU THE BOUGHS
AND VOW'D HOW BEST TO COURT HER.
NEW BLOSSOM IN HER CHEEKS
KNOWS MORE THAN SHE O'UGHTER.

GOOD 'EALTH TO FARMER'S SON
A-STANDING IDLY BY
HERE'S TO SWEAT UPON THE BROW
THE CIDER'S OVER THERE M' BOYS
VILL THE CUP AND DRINK IT NOW.

This last poem was specially commisioned by John Leach, the potter of Muchelney who was making a large three and a half pint, three handled Wassail Mug for Frank and Val Dale of Long Sutton. The poem was inscribed on the side of the mug which was christened in the tap room at Eli's, Huish Episcopi, on Sept 8th 1999. Both the first airing of the poem and the whetting of the mug were recorded for posterity by Alasdair Cross and Richard Uridge of *'Open Country'* Radio 4.

BIBLIOGRAPHY

Vinetum Brittanicum or A Treatise on Cider
John Worlidge Second enlarged edtn. London 1678

Cyder a Poem John Phillips 1708,
Printed for J Tonson in the Strand   3rd edtn 1727

Camden's Brittania first published in Latin 1586,
translated into English by Edmund Gibson 1695. Printed
at the Unicorn, West End of St Paul's and at the Black
Swan Paternoster Rows

**Treatise of Fruit Trees and The Spiritual Use of an
Orchard** Ralph Austen 1653

Sylva - Pomona John Evelyn 1664

Aphorisms on the New way of improving Cider
Richard Haines 1684

The Closet of Sir Kenelm Digby Knight Opened   1669
reprinted Prospect Books 1997

**Certain Philosophical preparations for Food and
Beverage for Sea-men, in their long voyage.**
Sir Henry Platt 1607 Wellcome Library

Some observations concerning the ordering of wines -
an 8 page paper: Christopher Merret deposited
@ The Royal Society 1662

Discourse & Discovery of Newfoundland - Richard
Whitbourne 1619/20 & 1622 Edited Gillian T. Cell
Hakluyt Society 1982

Herefordshire Orchards : a Pattern for all England
John Beale 1656

A Treatise on Cyder-making H Stafford London 1759

Treatise on Cider Thomas Andrew Knight 1797

Pomona Herefordiensis Thomas Andrew Knight 1811

A Book about Cider and Perry CW Radcliffe Cooke
London 1898

Cidermaking in Somerset   Phillipa Legg
Somerset Rural Life Museum, Glastonbury 1984

Somerset Cider : The Complete Story
Philipa Legg and Hilary Binding, Somerset Books 1999

The History and Virtues of Cyder RK French
Robert Hale 1982

Cider's Story - Rough & Smooth Mark Foot   1999

Cider in Folklore : WE Minchinton
Folklife XIII 1975

Cider in Europe WE Minchinton

The British cider Industry since 1870   WE Minchinton
National Westminster Quarterly Review 1975

Early Days of Cider Making   EP Bulmer
Museum of Cider 1996

Bulmers : A Century of Cidermaking LP Wilkinson
David & Charles 1987

Cider and Juice Apples - Growing and Processing
edited by RR Williams Long Ashton/ Bristol University
1988

A Drink for its Time Michael B Quinion
Museum of Cider Hereford 1979

Cidermaking Michael B Quinion
Shire Publications 1997

Cider & Scrumpy Bob Bunker Bossiney Books 1999

The Book of Apples Joan Morgan & Alison Richards
Ebury Press London 1993

The English Apple Rosanne Sanders
RHS / Phaidon Oxford 1988

The Apple Source Book Common Ground 1991

Apple Games & Customs Common Ground 1994

The Apple Map of England Common Ground

Orchards - A guide to Local Conservation
Common Ground 1989

Local Distinctiveness - Conference Essays
Common Ground 1993

A Calendar of Country Customs Ralph Whitlock
Batsford 1978

Devon Apples Andy Brown Maquette Press 1999

Dorsetshire Folklore John Udal   (1922)
reprinted Toucan Press Guernsey 1970

Dorset Dialect with a Grammar William Barnes (1886)
reprinted Toucan Press Guernsey 1970

Rural Life in Wessex 1500- 1900 JH Bettey
Moonraker Press 1977

Bound to the Soil : A social History of Dorset 1750-1918
Barbara Kerr 1968

Natural History of Wiltshire   John Aubrey (1688)
reprinted   1969

**John Aubrey and the Genesis of the Monumenta
Brittanica** now available in **Wormholes** : Essays and
occasional writings. by John Fowles Jonathan Cape 1998

The Tree John Fowles Aurum Press 1979
Sumach Press 1992

The Golden Bough JG Frazer Macmillan 1922

Ripest Apples Compiled by Roy Palmer
The Big Apple Association 1996

Gardens of Delight Miles & John Hadfield   Cassell 1964

Cooking Apples - Recipes from Ampleforth Abbey
Editor Caroline Miles   Gracewing 1982

Apples Frank Browning Allen Lane - Penguin 1999

The Prose of John Clare Edited by JW and Anne Tibble
RKP 1951

In Time of Flood - The Somerset Levels -
The River Parrett - James Crowden
The Parrett Trail Partnership 1996

Blood Earth & Medicine - A year in the life of a casual
agricultural labourer - James Crowden Parrett Press 1991

Champagne   Tom Stevenson
Christies / Absolute Press 1998

A Forest Journey - The role of Wood in the Development
of Civilisation John Perlin Harvard University Press 1991

Somerset - The Complete Guide   Robin Bush
Dovecote Press 1994

Acts of Parliament for continuing and granting to His
Majesty certain Duties upon Malt, Mum, Cyder and
Perry. 1710 - 1797

NOTES ON THE ILLUSTRATIONS

I cannot let the book end without saying a few words about '*Adam and Eve in Somerset*', the copper plate engraving on the cover, by Brian Hanscomb R.E. Brian is a very accomplished artist and for those wishing to see more of his work please contact him directly, but please phone first and make an appointment.

He lives @   Tor View, Limehead, St Breward, Bodmin, Cornwall. PL30 4LU.   Tel 01208 850806

As for the engraving I bought it many years ago from the artist. The image of Adam on his knees in the flowers, pleading with a Somerset Eve, who is being being more than usually coy, has always entertained me... as has the apple tree and the '*Samuel Palmer*' moon, or is it the last eclipse ? The hills are the rounded hills near Frome, between Temple Combe and Midsomer Norton, and the factory is the printworks at Paulton where Brian worked for many years as a gravure industrial engraver. Strangely enough one of the slang words for cider laced with gin is snake bite... As to the variety of apple and the eact nature of the relationship between Adam and Eve, I leave that to your imagination...

The illustration of '*The Great Cyder Press*' used as a frontispiece comes from *A Treatise on Cyder Making* by H. Stafford 1759. I found it in Richard Watkin's shop and it was printed on the back of a Gentleman's Magazine Almanac chart, showing the times of the sun rising and setting. Very useful... *The Great Cyder Press* is an interesting example of a Windlass Press, but I feel that the artist had only a slender idea of the work needed as the pressure is not exactly being exerted on the cheese. Although it could equally well be argued that the 'exploded' view gives you more idea of what is going on.

Another worker would have been needed the other side, also with a windlass, otherwise the threads would soon become jammed, crossed or worse still stripped. Capstans were popular and no doubt incorporated from the extensive nautical knowlege which must have existed in certain South coast cider-drinking ports...

The three illustrations I have used from John Worlidge's *Treatise on Cider* 1678, are also a great pleasure and show the nature of the work involved with the '*Ingenio*' the patent crusher through whose jaws the apples must first pass before being devoured by the press itself. Amazingly, devices very similar in design to this were still being made in the last century two hundred years later. It was a simple but portable device that two men could operate with ease, and the pomace comes out neatly at the bottom. Note the fine looking baskets and barrels. The farmer would surely have to get in good supplies of bread and cheese to keep them working round the clock...

As to the press, maybe this is a picture of John Worlidge himself... He certainly looks the part, and the great wooden thread must have taken some cutting out. Also I am intrigued by the basket system employed, through which the pressed apple juice runs. This one is also portable and can, as illustrated here, be used outside, which saves carting the apples all the way back to the farm, although it means you have to take the barrels back.

As to the small and rather eccentric initial woodblocks which have been used for enumerating the various chapters, they are taken from *Cider Acts of Parliament* which dealt with taxation on *Malt, Mum, Cyder and Perry* ranging from 1710 to 1797.   Mum was a type of beer made in Brunswick no doubt brought over by the

Hanoverians. Maybe it was the beginning of the Lager culture... The woodblocks were placed at the beginning part of the Act and were always set in pride of place. The gap in the middle meant that various different letters sould be substituted or as in this case numbers... The Acts of course informed the farmer or cider dealer that he owed 4/- or 6/- or even, as in 1763, 10/- a hogshead to the Revenue Men who were known to be ruthless... Towards the end of the 18th Cent the quality of the woodblocks tailed off and became very uninteresting, as they only showed the Royal Coat of Arms... It was as if they were the tail end of the illuminated manuscript era, when each starter letter was given extraordinary importance, and let the calligrapher, or in this case the wood block engraver, free range to show off his skills. Some from the 16th Cent and 17th Cent are superb...

Two other illustrations, *The Sun and Moon,* and the end piece *Bouquet* have been taken from John Phillips *Cyder - A Poem 1727 edition.*

Lastly the photograph of the *Cider Gang...* This was taken at Burrow Hill in 1995 but it might just have well been 1895... The workers are in characteristic pose. Guess which one is the author ?... On the left and holding onto the guard rail, which prevents you falling down into the wooden cider apple pit, is Bob Pride who was brought up round Tetbury in Gloucestershire. Bob has had a wide variety of jobs, but at the time this photograph was taken he was living in a 'bender' at the bottom of the orchard. He owned a small piece of land, about three acres, which was his inheritance, but he was not allowed to live on it, which was ironic as his grandfather's farm on the outskirts of Tetbury had been commandeered after the last war, by compulsory purchase to build council houses. Being realistic, he sold the land to the nextdoor neighbour and bought himself a small redbrick Victorian house in North Petherton, Somerset.

Next to Bob is the famous, or is it infamous ? *Pigeon Biter...* We call him *Pigeon* or *Biter* for short, he has a history of gamekeeping, long net rabbitting, hunting of all sorts, dog, breeding, donkey rides, story telling and more recently helping to present his own brand of blood thirsty cooking with TV Dinners on Channel No 4. I first met *Pigeon* in Bristol Docks when I was working on the Bristol Packet as a boatman... little realising then that I would spend a season or two chatting over the cheeses. His view of the world is an interesting one, he studied Modern History and philosophy at Bristol University during the student riot days... *Pigeon* now lives close by, within easy reach of the *Halfway House...*

Next to *Pigeon* is Chris King who at the time was 'Pit Boy' and was horsedrawn and living in his own bow top gipsy wagon. He had a marvellous heavy horse that went by the name of Scammell who could pull carts up hill at a cracking pace. I well remember the smell of hot leather and horse sweat. When his father died Chris inherited 20,000 cabbages near Ringwood and he had to harvest them and then sell them... His young son Eli is named after the publican of a local hostelry, the *Rose & Crown* at Huish Episcopi near Langport.

And then there is the author, who has worked at Burrow Hill more years than he can remember, starting off sheep shearing back in the early eighties... James was born in Plymouth in 1954 and grew up on the Western edge of Dartmoor, living mainly round Tavistock. After school he joined the army, read Civil Engineering at Bristol and then in 1976 'high-tailed' it to the Himalaya where he spent a winter in Zangskar. An extraordinary experience which he has yet to write up... After that he studied Anthropology at Oxford and then lived for a year in the Outer Hebrides before returning to Bristol where he

worked in the Docks as a boatman. Since then he has
been self-employed as a casual agricultural worker being
involved with sheep shearing, night lambing, forestry and
cidermaking. He has recently 'retired' from the land and is
now concentrating on writing full time.

His first book of poetry, '*Blood Earth & Medicine – a
year in the life of a casual agricultural labourer*' was
published in 1991. This has been translated into French by
Rene Agostini of Avignon University and will be
published later this year. This was followed in 1996 by
'*In Time of Flood – the Somerset Levels – the River Parrett*'
with photographs by George Wright.
His next book called *South Crofty – The Wheal of Hope*
concerns the plight of the last working Cornish Tin Mine
which shut in March 1998, as well as the history of hard
rock mining in Cornwall and its human impact on the
population. 30 poems and copious historical notes are
accompanied by George Wright's pictures. James still
lives and works in Somerset.

The illustration of an apple at the beginning of the book is
of the famous *Redstreak*, taken from a post card bought at
the Museum of Cider, and this image was in turn taken
from a painting by Miss Alice Ellis from "*Herefordshire
Pomona*" 1876-1885. It is included at the beginning of the
book as a mark of respect to Lord Scudamore, John
Worlidge and John Phillips who did so much to raise the
awareness of Cyder.

The Cider House Gang - Burrow Hill 1995

CIDER PRODUCERS & PLACES OF INTEREST

This is by no means an exhaustive list, but it should be good enough to be getting on with, the order is slightly random but that should make it more interesting :

 THE SOMERSET CIDER BRANDY COMPANY & BURROW HILL CIDER Pass Vale Farm, Burrow Hill, Kingsbury Episcopi, Martock, Somerset TA12 5BU
Tel & Fax 01460 240782
or if you have got webbed feet   www.ciderbrandy.co.uk

PERRY BROS CIDER MILLS,
Orchardland, Dowlish Wake. Ilminster, Somerset
01460 52681

SHEPPY'S CIDER FARM CENTRE
Three Bridges, Bradford-on-Tone, Taunton, Somerset
Tel 01823 461233   Fax 01823 461712

THATCHER'S CIDER Company Ltd.
Myrtle Farm, Station Rd, Sandford, Churchill, Somerset
01934 822862

RICH'S FARMHOUSE CIDER
Mill Farm, Watchfield, Highbridge, Somerset TA9 4RD
Tel 01278 783651 Fax 01278 786651

COOMBE'S CIDER
Japonica farm, Mark Causeway Highbridge,
Somerset TA9 4QD   O1278 641265

BRIDGE FARM CIDER
East Chinnock, Nr Crewkerne, Somerset

HECKS FARMHOUSE CIDER
9-11 Middle Leigh, Street, Somerset
01769 572678

ROGER WILKINS CIDER
Mudgley, Wedmore, Somerset.

COUNTRYMAN CIDER
Felldownhead, Bradstone, Tavistock
01822 870226

GRAY's FARM CIDER
Halstow, Tedburn St. Mary, Exeter Devon
01647 61236

**GOSPEL GREEN CHEESE
& CHAMPAGNE   CIDER MAKERS**
Gospel Green Cottage, Gospel Green
Haslemere, Surrey GU27 3BH
01428 654120

GREEN VALLEY CYDER Ltd
Darts Farm, Clyst St George,
Exeter, Devon EX3 0QH

DUNKERTON'S CIDER
Hays Head, Luntley Leominster, Herefordshire HR6 9ED
01544 388653

H WESTON & SONS Ltd
The Bounds, Much Marcle, Ledbury, Herefordshire
01531 660233

SYMOND'S CIDER & ENGLISH WINE Co.Ltd.
The Cider Mill, Stoke Lacy, Bromyard
Herefordshire, HR7 4HG   01885 490411

HEREFORD CIDER MUSEUM
& KING OFFA DISTILLERY
21 Ryelands St. Hereford
01432 354027

THE ENGLISH FARM CIDER CENTRE
Middle Farm,Firle, Lewes Sussex
01323 811411

BROGDALE HORTICULTURAL TRUST
Brogdale Rd, Faversham, Kent
01795 535286/535462

CHARLTON ORCHARDS
Charlton Rd, Creech St. Michael, Taunton Somerset
01823 412959 / 412979

NEW CROSS FRUIT FARM Ltd
West Lambrook, South Petherton. Somerset
01460 241641

VIGO Ltd (for a whole range pressing Eqt etc etc)
& BOLHAYES CIDER : Unit 2, Station Rd Industrial
Estate, Hemyock, Devon   Tel 01823 680230

COMMON GROUND
PO Box 25309 London NW5 1ZA

BIGWOOD & STAPLE   Printers
The Mill, Church Street, Bridgwater Somerset.
Tel : 01278 424014   Fax : 01278 429586

BROWN & FORREST
Smoked eel, duck, cheese, ham, salmon,chicken etc etc.
Mail Order a speciality The Smokery, Bowden's farm,
Hambridge, Langport, Somerset   01458 251520

JOHN LEACH   Potter
Muchelney Pottery, Muchelney, near Langport, Somerset
01458 250324

MUCHELNEY ABBEY   Muchelney Nr Langport.
01458 250664 Open 1st April - 30th October 10 - 6

SOMERSET RURAL LIFE MUSEUM
Abbey Farm, Chilkwell St, Glastonbury BA6 8DB
01458 831197 Opening Hours: Summer Tues - Fri 10-5
Sat & Sun 2-6pm   Winter Tues - Sat 10-3

CYDER PRESS 2
The Old Parsonage, Somerton, Somerset TA11 7PF   UK
For distribution please contact :
TOR MARK, United Downs Industrial Estate, St Day,
Redruth. Cornwall. Tel : 01209 822101

THE CYDER PRESS AND BINDERY NZ.
For high quality fine bookbinding, gold tooling
& leathercraft. Contact the proprieter Roger Crowden....
Sunbeamland, Taumerere, Nr. Kawakawa,
Northland, New Zealand.
Post : C/0 P.O. OPUA, Northland, NZ
Tel & Fax from UK 00 649 404 0154

Bigwood and Staple is a long established family firm that combines the excellence of a fine printing tradition with the most modern of design skills. Alfred Bigwood started the firm in the middle of the last century and in 1883 he took on an apprentice, Frederick Staple at 1/- a week. By 1894 Frederick had taken over the business and it has been in the family ever since. The premises of Bigwood & Staple are at Bridgwater in an old grain mill on the east bank of the River Parrett.

Cider : the Forgotten Miracle is set in Adobe Caslon and Zapf Chancery. It was printed with offset litho machines at Bigwood and Staple in Bridgwater during October 1999. The paper is 135 gsm Elan cream.

THE END.